ILSE MINTZ

The Catholic University of America and

National Bureau of Economic Research

Dating postwar business cycles:

METHODS AND THEIR APPLICATION
TO WESTERN GERMANY, 1950–67

OCCASIONAL PAPER 107

National Bureau of Economic Research

New York 1969

Distributed by Columbia University Press

New York and London

National Bureau of Economic Research

187172

RELATION OF THE DIRECTORS TO THE WORK AND PUBLICATIONS
OF THE NATIONAL BUREAU OF ECONOMIC RESEARCH

1. The object of the National Bureau of Economic Research is to ascertain and to present to the public important economic facts and their interpretation in a scientific and impartial manner. The Board of Directors is charged with the responsibility of ensuring that the work of the National Bureau is carried on in strict conformity with this object.

2. The President of the National Bureau shall submit to the Board of Directors, or to its Executive Committee, for their formal adoption all specific proposals for research to be instituted.

3. No research report shall be published until the President shall have submitted to each member of the Board the manuscript proposed for publication, and such information as will, in his opinion and in the opinion of the author, serve to determine the suitability of the report for publication in accordance with the principles of the National Bureau. Each manuscript shall contain a summary drawing attention to the nature and treatment of the problem studied, the character of the data and their utilization in the report, and the main conclusions reached.

4. For each manuscript so submitted, a special committee of the Board shall be appointed by majority agreement of the President and Vice Presidents (or by the Executive Committee in case of inability to decide on the part of the President and Vice Presidents), consisting of three directors selected as nearly as may be one from each general division of the Board. The names of the special manuscript committee shall be stated to each Director when the manuscript is submitted to him. It shall be the duty of each member of the special manuscript committee to read the manuscript. If each member of the manuscript committee signifies his approval within thirty days of the transmittal of the manuscript, the report may be published. If at the end of that period any member of the manuscript committee withholds his approval, the President shall then notify each member of the Board, requesting approval or disapproval of publication, and thirty days additional shall be granted for this purpose. The manuscript shall then not be published unless at least a majority of the entire Board who shall have voted on the proposal within the time fixed for the receipt of votes shall have approved.

5. No manuscript may be published, though approved by each member of the special manuscript committee, until forty-five days have elapsed from the transmittal of the report in manuscript form. The interval is allowed for the receipt of any memorandum of dissent or reservation, together with a brief statement of his reasons, that any member may wish to express; and such memorandum of dissent or reservation shall be published with the manuscript if he so desires. Publication does not, however, imply that each member of the Board has read the manuscript, or that either members of the Board in general or the special committee have passed on its validity in every detail.

6. Publications of the National Bureau issued for informational purposes concerning the work of the Bureau and its staff, or issued to inform the public of activities of Bureau staff, and volumes issued as a result of various conferences involving the National Bureau shall contain a specific disclaimer noting that such publication has not passed through the normal review procedures required in this resolution. The Executive Committee of the Board is charged with review of all such publications from time to time to ensure that they do not take on the character of formal research reports of the National Bureau, requiring formal Board approval.

7. Unless otherwise determined by the Board or exempted by the terms of paragraph 6, a copy of this resolution shall be printed in each National Bureau publication.

(Resolution adopted October 25, 1926, and revised February 6, 1933,
February 24, 1941, and April 20, 1968)

Acknowledgements

My greatest debt is to Geoffrey H. Moore who helped me generously at every step with his unmatched expertise and unfailing judgment. Arthur F. Burns' suggestions concerning the general direction of the study also were invaluable.

I further wish to acknowledge the many helpful comments made by the members of the Staff Reading Committee, Gerhard Bry, Raymond Goldsmith and Victor Zarnowitz.

Many thanks are due to Dennis Thornton who assisted me with enthusiasm and ingenuity, to Charlotte Boschan who developed and supervised the computer programs and to Richard Ruggles who produced the appendix tables. I am grateful to Hanna Stern who most carefully checked the data, to Haim Dori who helped the manuscript through its later stages, and to Irving Forman for expert work on the charts. Mrs. Gouldin deserves thanks for an excellent editing job.

The German Economic Institute, Berlin, assisted me greatly by providing some of the basic data.

Contents

Tables

Charts

Foreword

Nearly twenty years ago Arthur Burns described an "unseen" cycle underlying the swings in aggregate economic activity. As he put it:

A continual transformation of the economic system occurs beneath the surface phenomena of aggregate expansion and contraction .... There are two cycles in economic activity, not one. First, there is the cycle of sustained expansions and contractions in the aggregate itself. Second, there is the cycle in the distributions of expansions and contractions within the aggregate. The first cycle is "seen" since we are accustomed to following comprehensive records of business conditions. The second cycle is "unseen" since few of us subject the components of comprehensive aggregates to close examination.[1]

Ilse Mintz has now demonstrated the existence of a similar type of "unseen" cycle in an economy where the usual type of "seen" cycle has not been highly visible. After World War II and until 1966, aggregate economic activity in West Germany grew almost uninterruptedly. The "cycle of sustained expansions and contractions in the aggregate" was not apparent in comprehensive measures of activity such as the gross national product or total employment. This ordinarily visible sign of the business cycle had dropped from sight. But the "cycle in the distributions of expansions and contractions within the aggregate" had, as Mrs. Mintz shows, not been eliminated.

Two statistical techniques, applied quite independently to various significant measures of economic activity, reveal sustained periods when economic activity in Germany grew at an abnormally high rate, alternating with sustained periods when activity grew at an abnormally low rate. Relative to the long-term growth, general expansions and contractions similar to those experienced before World War II in Germany and in other countries continued to occur. Armed with these results, Mrs. Mintz proceeds to establish a chronology setting forth the beginning and ending dates of these "expansions" and "contractions," which she calls "speedups" and "slowdowns."

Her work puts into operational form a concept of the business cycle that is both old and new. The idea that a business cycle can be measured as a short-term deviation from a long-term trend was developed in the work of

---

[1] *New Facts on Business Cycles,* 30th Annual Report of the NBER, May 1950, pp. 10-11 (reprinted in *The Business Cycle in a Changing World,* New York, NBER, 1969.)

Henry L. Moore, Warren M. Persons, Frederick R. Macaulay, Edwin Frickey and others during 1910-30.[2] Then for several decades this view of the business cycle was almost ignored. The Great Depression and the boom accompanying World War II made secular trend measurement both difficult and hardly necessary for the purpose of discerning cycles. Econometric model builders generally shunned the idea of separating trend and cycle.

Recently, however, there has been a resurgence of interest, especially in analyzing the gap between actual and potential output. The potential output is that calculated to result under conditions of full employment, and hence it is governed by the long-run trends in the labor force, the average workweek and productivity. The deviation of actual output from this full employment trend level is the "gap." This analysis differs from some of the earlier work in its fuller development of the theoretical basis for the level of potential output and its rate of change, although the results still depend importantly upon extrapolative procedures.[3] Various measures of capacity utilization are similar in concept, and all of them bear a resemblance to the "deviation from trend" idea.

Mrs. Mintz uses deviations from trend explicitly as one method of identifying cycles. The alternative method, following the work of Friedman and Schwartz, identifies alternating periods of "high" and "low" rates of growth, without reference to an explicit trend. Applied to individual series, the two methods do not always yield the same set of cycles or identical dates. But the similarities predominate, and the upshot is strikingly consistent evidence of a widely diffused cyclical movement in the German economy. On this basis Mrs. Mintz is able to firmly establish a chronology of business cycles in West Germany from 1951 to 1967.

The American reader of this study is likely to ask: What implications do these results have for the United States? More than eight years have passed

---

[2] For an account of this development up the mid-twenties, see Wesley C. Mitchell, *Business Cycles: The Problem and Its Setting,* New York, NBER, 1927, pp. 190-233. This work also contains many examples of indexes of business activity adjusted for secular trend (including one for Germany, 1898-1914)and develops a chronology of U.S. business cycles based upon five such indexes (see p. 335). The effect of trend adjustment upon cyclical measures is explored more thoroughly in *Measuring Business Cycles* by Arthur F. Burns and Wesley C. Mitchell, New York, NBER, 1946.

[3] In this connection it is interesting to recall Wesley Mitchell's view on secular trends in his 1927 volume on business cycles:

We stand to learn more about economic oscillations at large and about business cycles in particular, if we approach the problem of trends as theorists, than if we confine ourselves to strictly empirical work. The trends which promise the most important additions to our knowledge are those which correspond to rational hypotheses, although they may not "fit the data" so well as empirical constructions which are difficult to interpret. For it may prove possible to integrate the rational hypotheses which yield instructive trends with the theory of business cycles (p. 230).

since the last business cycle turning point, in February 1961. Have business cycles of the type formerly identified disappeared? Would Mrs. Mintz' procedures, applied to U.S. data, bring them to light? Should we henceforth use her methods to develop a business cycle chronology for the United States?

The application of these methods to data for the United States as well as for other countries is, indeed, a part of the present investigation. Pending its completion, we can only speculate upon the nature of the results. In the first place, the peak dates would likely be earlier than the present business cycle peaks, and the trough dates may be later. Such shifts are not inevitable, since they depend on how sharply defined the movements in activity are in the neighborhood of the present dates, and they may affect peaks more than troughs or vice versa. But the upshot is likely to be a more nearly equal division of the cycle into expansion and contraction phases than is presently the case: expansions or speedups would be shorter and contractions or slowdowns longer.

Furthermore, some contraction phases may be recognized where none are now, and those that were marginal in terms of the present concept would become clearer. The slower rates of growth in early 1967, in late 1962 and early 1963, in 1956 and in 1951-52, for example, would become candidates for admission to the list of business cycle contractions.

These speculations about the nature of the results raise some questions of their own. Would the list of cycles, and their dates, become as generally accepted as the present chronology? Would they be more dependent upon the particular statistical technique used to identify them? More dependent upon the judgment of the investigator? Would there be greater uncertainty and hence a longer lag in identifying downturns or upturns promptly than is presently the case? Should the present chronology be continued in addition to the new one? If so, would the existence of two chronologies be a source of confusion, since at times they may appear inconsistent?

The basic question, of course, is whether a new chronology of business cycles will be an aid to analysis. There can be little doubt that it will. Since Thorp's pioneering work for the National Bureau, which first established business cycle chronologies for many countries,[4] the analytical value of such chronologies has become generally recognized. Not only is the U.S. chronology widely used in government and private publications and reports, but similar work has recently been undertaken for other countries (e.g., Canada, Japan, Italy, Great Britain and Australia). Such chronologies provide benchmarks, facilitating all sorts of comparisons. With the computer programs that are now available, both to aid in establishing the chronologies

---

[4] Willard L. Thorp, *Business Annals,* NBER, 1926.

and in analyzing data in terms of them, an ever-widening use lies ahead. We shall have reason, therefore, to be grateful to Mrs. Mintz for providing a new tool for exploring the causes and consequences of business cycles, and for examining the achievements of economic policy in dealing with them.

Geoffrey H. Moore

The definition of the business cycle revisited

In April 1967 an international conference of economists was held in London to discuss the topic: "Is the Business Cycle Obsolete?" One of the participants, Geoffrey H. Moore, answered: "The question posed by this conference may be obsolete, the problem of booms and recessions is not."[1] This view, that business cycles are not extinct, should receive strong support from the findings of the present paper as a glance at the German cycles in Chart 1 will show.

The reason for suspecting the demise of the business cycle is the mildness of most recent business recessions in most countries. In the words of Arthur F. Burns: "the business cycle has become milder as a result of a favorable conjuncture of structural changes and of both better and wider understanding of the requirements of business cycle policy. . . . Even before World War II, the business cycle was a milder type of fluctuation in western Europe than in the United States, and the difference has persisted in the postwar period."[2] Periods regarded as downswings by business and policy makers in Europe and Japan have not usually been characterized by declines in aggregate output, income or employment. Rather they are periods of retardation in the rate of growth of the economy.

Since recent economic fluctuations are, in some respects, unlike earlier ones, it is not surprising that views on the persistence or disappearance of business cycles vary with the importance an observer attaches to these contrasts as opposed to the equally undeniable likenesses.

Those who regard an absolute decline in the main economic activities as an essential feature of business cycles, see a deep gap between earlier and recent economic fluctuations. A mere retardation in output growth is, in their opinion, entirely different in nature from a fall in output. Retardations, they argue, have been observed at all times, but have not previously been put into the same class as declines in activity and this distinction should quite definitely be retained. These adherents of the classical business cycle must conclude either that business cycles are more or less a thing of the past in

---

[1] "Is the Business Cycle Obsolete?" Conference organized by the Social Science Research Council and held in London, England, April 1967 (referred to below as "London conference"). Geoffrey H. Moore's discussion of R. A. Gordon's paper, mimeographed, p. 1.

[2] Arthur F. Burns, *The Business Cycle in a Changing World.*

many countries; or that the last two decades were exceptional and that the classical business cycle will reappear.

A second group of economists takes a somewhat different position. They agree with the first group that absolute rises and declines are essential, but they compromise by accepting declines in selected activities in lieu of declines in aggregate activity as a criterion for business cycle recessions. Absolute declines may occur in certain economic indicators even in periods of rising total income, output and employment. These will be indicators which, for one reason or another, do not reflect the general upward trend or indicators which experience cyclical swings with amplitudes so large that absolute falls occur despite such a trend. A period of decline in such indicators can, in this view, be defined as a period of recession despite the continued growth in the rest of the economy.

The switch from decline in aggregate activity to decline in selected activities involves a more radical change in concept than may appear at first. The revised concept can be defended only on one of two assumptions: either the activities selected for their absolute declines are more significant than those not declining; or else the absolute decline in selected activities coincides with reduced growth in the rest of the economy and is significant for this reason. Even if this last assumption should be warranted, the criterion for recession is actually shifted from absolute decline to slow growth.

The concept of the business cycle described above has not been explicitly stated and advocated, as far as I know. Nor have the underlying assumptions been spelled out and investigated. Yet empirical business cycle research in some countries is based on it. The reason is probably that it retains the classical direction-of-change criterion and requires no revision of statistical methods in contrast to the modified concept discussed below. However, this simplicity is more apparent than real in view of the crucial unanswered questions mentioned above.

The third business cycle concept, which is widely accepted today and which is the basis of the present paper, sees the crucial aspect of the business cycle in the *difference* between the behavior of the economy in two types of periods. The nature and significance of this difference are essentially the same, it claims, whether the rates of change are positive in both phases - as they may be in a rapidly growing economy - or whether the rates of change have alternate signs as is likely in a more slowly growing economy. There is no good reason why alternations between periods of, say, 2-per cent rises and of l-per cent falls (which could qualify as a classical business cycle) should be entirely different in nature from alternations between periods of, say, 4-per cent rises and l-per cent rises.

The similarity of the classical and the revised concepts may appear even more clearly when alternations of high and low growth rates are viewed as cycles in trend adjusted economic activities. In their fundamental work on business cycles, Burns and Mitchell stated that ideally business cycle analysis should rest on two sets of measures - with and without secular trends. The high cost of double analysis (in precomputer times) prevented them from undertaking it.[3] The analysis of trend adjusted data may thus be regarded as a continuation of the analysis initiated in *Measuring Business Cycles.*

The widened concept requires only a minor amendment of the Burns and Mitchell definition of business cycles which underlies the National Bureau's cycle analysis. The definition speaks of "expansions occurring at about the same time in many economic activities followed by similarly general .,. . contractions . . . ."[4] Here the words "adjusted for their long-run trends," have to be inserted. When long-run trends are horizontal, there will, of course, be no difference between the two versions of the concept. The view that there is close resemblance in duration, pervasiveness and other aspects, between classical business cycles and cycles in trend adjusted data will be supported by the findings of this study.

This view is shared by some of the foremost experts in the field. For instance, in the paper he presented at the aforementioned London conference R. A. Gordon asked: "Can we say that business cycles exist if a country experiences 'recurring alternations' of acceleration and retardation in the rate of growth of output and employment rather than alternating expansions and contractions in the absolute level of these and other important variables?"

And he answered: "I should answer this question in the affirmative. If we find regular (but not necessarily periodic) swings in rates of growth and if these swings are of roughly the same duration and are associated with many of the same phenomena (such as cyclical changes in interest rates, the balance of trade, cost-price relations, and unemployment) as was the case with past fluctuations that we did call business cycles, then I should be inclined to say that these 'growth cycles' should be called 'business cycles'."[5]

---

[3] "Doubtless the ideal procedure would be to make two sets of measures for each series: one set based on the original data adjusted only for seasonal variations, as is our present practice, the other based on the best attainable isolation of the 'cyclical component' of the data. But the resources at our disposal place grave obstacles to the realization of this ideal." Arthur F. Burns and Wesley C. Mitchell, *Measuring Business Cycles,* NBER, 1946.

[4] The full definition is: "Business cycles are a type of fluctuation found in the aggregate economic activity of nations that organize their work mainly in business enterprises: a cycle consists of expansions occurring at about the same time in many economic activities, followed by similarly general recessions, contractions, and revivals which merge into the expansion phase of the next cycle; this sequence of changes is recurrent but not periodic; in duration business cycles vary from more than one year to ten or twelve years; they are not divisible into shorter cycles of similar character with amplitudes approximating their own." *Ibid.,* p. 3.

[5] R. A. Gordon, "The Stability of the American Economy," London conference, mimeographed, pp. 1, 2.

A similar view was expressed by R. C. O. Matthews reporting on Britain: "Cyclical movements in the British economy in the postwar period have been at least as clear-cut and regular as they were in earlier times . . . . But . . . no postwar year has shown a significant decline in real GDP. Fluctuations have taken the form of fluctuations in the growth rate."[6]

The German literature on business cycles also regards this definition as valid. In the words of Erich Preiser: For "the trade cycle policy maker of the old school there were upswings and downswings, peaks and troughs, and the statistician measured the amplitude of fluctuations as the distance from a horizontal datum line. Nowadays the very terminology makes it clear that the trade cycle is regarded as the motion pattern of a growing economy."[7]

The following statements by experts of the International Monetary Fund, are further examples of the indicated views. Says Rudolf R. Rhomberg: "Declines in economic activity in industrial countries have been rare, and business cycle analysts have had to direct their attention to periodic advances and retardations of growth rates - or periods of expansions and of pause - rather than to actual booms and recessions of the old-fashioned kind." And David Williams writes: "Indeed, the European economy as a whole - i.e., the economy of the 19 European countries which comprise the Organization for Economic Cooperation and Development (OECD) - has been virtually free of the regular cyclical behavior that has characterized the U.S. economy and, even more strikingly, the interwar period of 1919-39 . . . . There have been six recessions in economic activity in the European economy . . . of which only three . . . have shown marked retardations in the rate of growth, and declines in industrial production. During the other three recessions . . . the decline in the rate of growth of output and demand was very slight." It is noteworthy that Williams designates as recessions even periods with fairly rapid growth in aggregate output and demand.[8]

Casual references to periods of low growth as "recessions" abound in the literature. For one example: the British National Institute's *Economic Review* speaks of "France . . . recovering from a recession" with reference to an increase in the rate of growth of French industrial production from 2 per cent to 7 per cent.[9]

---

[6]R.C.O. Matthews, "Postwar Business Cycles in the United Kingdom," London conference, mimeographed, p. 1.

[7]Erich Preiser, "Economic Growth as a Fetish and a Necessity," *German Economic Review,* 1967, no. 4.

[8]Rudolf R. Rhomberg, "Transmission of Business Fluctuations from Developed to Developing Countries," *International Monetary Fund Staff Papers,*March 1968, p. 1. David Williams, "What's Left of the Business Cycle in Europe?" International Monetary Fund and International Bank for Reconstruction and Development, *Finance and Development,*Washington, D.C., March 1968, p. 42.

[9]National Institute of Economic and Social Research, *Economic Review,* August 1966, p. 27.

As to business, policy makers and the general public, aspirations have risen with achievements here as in other fields. Once used to greater stability, people pay as much attention to fluctuations in growth rates as they previously bestowed on classical business cycles. Periods of low growth are, in Europe at least, commonly referred to as "recessions." When, for instance, the growth of industrial production and GNP had slowed down but not yet turned into decline, in the autumn of 1966, the German press spoke of a "deep descent." The German Economic Institute commented: "At present, at any rate, deep pessimism prevails," and it referred to generally "disastrous reports from businesses and regions."[10]

In sum, it seems to me that the question of where to draw the line between the phases of the business cycle is a matter of classification, and as in all such matters there is no right or wrong answer but only a more or less useful one. Distinguishing between two types of periods of differing economic experience, i.e., between business cycle phases, has proved eminently useful for the analysis of economic change. But this usefulness is diminished when one of the two phases occurs quite rarely and briefly. As long as absolute declines are frequent, drawing the line between absolute rises and falls is a most fruitful distinction. But when absolute declines are an exception, a different dividing line becomes more useful.

However, in accepting the concept of alternating higher and lower growth rates one must be fully aware of its important implications for economic policies. In fact, such policy implications may be an important reason for arguing that cycles around a horizontal trend are fundamentally different from those around a rising trend. "A cycle defined as an alternation of algebraically higher and lower rates of growth does not have simple implications for policy. For instance, mere reduction in the rate of growth of aggregate economic activity may not warrant an anti-recession policy."[11] Undoubtedly, considerable disagreement among experts is to be expected in regard to cycles around a rising trend. Should policies aim at some particular growth rate? And if so, at which one? Expressions such as "easing of pressures," "cooling-off periods," and so on, suggest that it is not always the highest possible rate which is considered the most desirable. Designating the aim as the highest rate compatible with price stability also is not likely to lead to uncontroversial classification of the actual situations. But, experts differ just as well in their positions on classical business cycles. Those favoring rapid growth even at the cost of inflation recommend expansive policies, not only

---

[10]"Zur Zeit jedenfalls herrscht tiefer Pessimismus." " ... Hiobsbotschaften von Unternehmen und Regionen ... ," Deutsches Institut fuer Wirtschaftsforschung, *Vierteljahrshefte zur Wirtschaftsforschung,* Berlin, 1966, Drittes Heft, pp. 255, 258.

[11]Moore, discussion of R.A. Gordon's paper, p. 4.

during recessions but also during slow expansions. On the other hand, those who consider inflation a greater evil than slow growth regard an occasional mild recession favorably.

These differences in viewpoint are similar to those found when declines are relative instead of absolute. The anti-inflationist view which regards boom periods with disfavor may, of course, be more prevalent with the greater frequency of such periods. Thus some German experts reserve their favorable adjectives for the slowdown when the economy is "on the way to the recovery of internal and external economic stability," while high growth phases are periods of "imbalance" and "overstraining." But such attitudes are not new and whether they are more or less frequent is again a matter of degree.

It would thus be desirable to introduce entirely value-free terms for the phases of business cycles. One might, for instance, speak of the x-phase and the y-phase. To avoid such strange language, I will use the terms speedup and slowdown for periods of above and below average growth. These terms will, I hope, be understood as implying no judgment on the desirability of one phase over the other.

Before closing the introductory comments, another disclaimer may be in order. The present paper does not deal with the causes of business cycles. Determining turning points does not any more conflict with the view that cycles are "managed," i.e., caused by government policies, than it conflicts with the view that these fluctuations are endogenous.

Methods of dating business cycles

If there is agreement on the continued existence of business cycles, the usefulness of dating them will hardly be challenged. Points of reference are indispensable for the measurement and, thus, for the analysis of changes during business cycles. We all have become so used to relying on the NBER chronology for the United States that we take this tool for granted.

A few other countries also fill this need. In Canada, Italy and Japan business cycle turning points are currently identified by official agencies. Two special studies provide dates for Australia, 1948-64; and at least the 1947-59 cycles for Britain have been dated.[12]

It is noteworthy that the NBER methods are used in all five of these chronologies. Those for Britain and Canada are based on the classical concept of the business cycle; the others on modified versions, although this is not stated explicitly. In the Italian and Japanese cases the selection of indicators is adjusted in such a way that a period may be classified as recession despite the absence of decline in aggregate output, income and employment. In Mallyon's analysis of Australian business cycles "an attempt was made to abstract from the trend component" in series with strong trends.

An explicit application of a widened cycle concept is used by Waterhouse in the second, especially ingenious, Australian study. Here various

---

[12]Peak and trough dates for Canada are given currently in *Current Statistical Indicators,* Department of Trade and Commerce, Ottawa (restricted).

Italian turning points are published by the Instituto Nazionale per lo Studio della Congiuntura, (ISCO), Rome, in *Rapporto al Consiglio Nazionale dell' Economia e del Lavoro.*

The Japanese chronology is in *Business Cycle Indicators,* Economic Planning Agency, Tokyo, and the trend adjusted chronology in Miyohei Shinohara, *Growth and Cycles in the Japanese Economy,* 1962, p. 153.

For Australia, dates for 1948-64 are provided in J.S. Mallyon, "Statistical Indicators of the Australian Trade Cycle," *Australian Economic Papers,* June 1966. Dates for trend adjusted cycles are in A.M.C. Waterman, "The Timing of Economic Fluctuations in Australia, January 1948 to December 1964," *Australian Economic Papers,* June 1967.

Business Cycle turning points for Great Britain, 1947-59, are found in C. Drakatos, "Leading Indicators for the British Economy," *National Institute Economic Review,* National Institute for Economic and Social Research, London, May 1963.

It should also be noted that British, French, and German business cycles before World War II have been dated at the NBER. See Burns and Mitchell, *Measuring Business Cycles.*

ways of dating turning points are explored and peaks and troughs in trend adjusted data are identified. The Bank of Japan also has derived a chronology from trend adjusted data.

For the majority of countries, however, business cycles have not been dated. This goes for Germany although its Economic Research Institute recognizes the desirability of such a tool when it notes: "Business cycle research is concerned with the modes of economic behavior. Comparison of activities requires analogous situations. Analogous situations have to be marked off."[13] One might expect this to be followed by a chronology, or at least the promise of a chronology. But all that follows is a discussion of the merits of different, somewhat vaguely circumscribed dates for the latest downturn.

In attempting to fill this gap the present paper employs, for a considerable part of the way, the methods used by the NBER in dating classical business cycles. First of all, we use the method of basing the reference cycle turns on turns in a considerable number of aggregative time series representing a broad array of economic processes. The alternative would be to rely on a single aggregate or index. One reason for preferring a wide variety of evidence is that this reduces the likelihood of error. Equating reference turns with GNP turns, as has sometimes been suggested, seems undesirable in view of the uncertainties in the measurement of GNP, the frequency of revisions and the quarterly time unit. These arguments are even more cogent for foreign countries than for the United States. Official German national income account data are available only annually. The German Economic Institute prepares quarterly interpolations which are subject to frequent and sizeable revisions. Although these quarterly data are included in our indicators, it does not seem advisable to base a quarterly chronology solely on one such series. A monthly chronology can obviously not be obtained in this fashion.[14]

There is, further, no reason to change the NBER rules that a full business cycle must have a minimum duration of more than a year. In specific series, cycles as short as fifteen months are recognized, though the shortest

---

[13]"Konjunkturforschung fragt nach Verhaltensweisen. Ein Vergleich von Verhaltensweisen verlangt analoge Situationen. Analoge Situationen muessen abgesteckt werden." Deutshes Institut fuer Wirtschaftsforschung, p. 254.

[14]For further arguments against reliance upon a single measure of total activity, see Geoffrey H. Moore, "What is a Recession?" *The American Statistician,* October 1967; and two articles by Victor Zarnowitz, "On the Dating of Business Cycles" and "Cloos on Reference Dates and Leading Indicators: A Comment," *The Journal of Business of the University of Chicago,* April and October 1963, respectively.

For a contrary view, see George W. Cloos, "How Good Are the National Bureau's Reference Dates?" *Journal of Business,* January 1963.

business cycle observed historically in the U.S. was seventeen months. While no minimum length for a business cycle phase has been laid down, in practice no phase shorter than six months has been recognized. Regarding amplitudes and diffusion no specific requirements have been set up in the NBER procedure, although the general requirement is imposed that cycles should be widely diffused and not be divisible into shorter cycles of similar character with amplitudes approximating their own.

So far, then, the dating of recent European business cycles encounters the same problems as the dating of classical U.S. business cycles. First, it must be decided whether or not a turning point has occurred; second, the precise month of the turn must be selected.[15] These problems are aggravated when we deal with foreign countries, however, because we are not helped by a long and generally accepted historical chronology. Decisions thus cannot be based on historical comparisons of durations, amplitudes and diffusion.

In addition, new statistical procedures must be devised in order to deal with the revised cycle concept. The two phases of the classical business cycle are distinguished by the *direction* of movement in aggregate economic activity. During an expansion the level of activity is rising and during a contraction it is falling. The revised cycle concept requires revision of this criterion.

Two methods are used in this study to cope with this problem. One is to adjust economic series for their long-run trends and to treat the deviations from these trends (deviation cycles) in the same fashion in which unadjusted data are treated in the analysis of classical cycles.

The second approach treats the percentage rate of change from month to month, or quarter to quarter, rather than the series proper, as the basic object of analysis. This is similar to the first approach in eliminating trends, but differs from it in requiring a special technique, as will be explained. The resulting cycles are termed step cycles.

With either method the turning dates will reflect the business cycle concept used, i.e., they will delimit periods of above and below average growth. Hence, in those instances in which an absolute decline in activity has occurred, they will tend to differ from dates selected on the basis of the classical business cycle concept. Downturns will come earlier, upturns later in trend adjusted series with upward trends than in unadjusted series. Therefore upswings will be shorter and downswings longer than in classical cycles.

---

[15] Even when the evidence does not clearly point to a single month, we choose as best we can. Otherwise it would be necessary to work with alternative turns or with turning zones, which would greatly reduce the usefulness of the chronology.

German indicators

In selecting indicators of German business cycles I was guided primarily by the list of roughly coincident indicators for the United States, i.e., indicators that have been found to turn at about the same time as business cycles. Since our concern is the determination of historical business cycle turning points, not the forecasting of future ones, indicators characterized by long leads at business turns are not included as a rule. This explains the exclusion of such cyclically sensitive series as orders, business intentions, etc.

A very large number of German economic time series is currently available. But, unfortunately, most are not in the shape required for my purposes. Many do not reach back as far as 1950 and those that do usually have breaks at the time of the incorporation of the Saarland into Western Germany and again at the time of the incorporation of West Berlin.

Analysis of the period at the beginning or end of a series is unavoidably surrounded by considerable uncertainty. Therefore coverage back to 1950 is indispensable for our purposes. The eighteen-year span that this provides is a minimum. Using a series in two or more segments is also out of the question. This would bring ends of series into the middle of the period and thus would greatly reduce the reliability of results that we obtain with continuous series for most of the period.

Thus, several series that would otherwise have been included in our list had to be omitted either because they were too short or because splicing factors for their various segments could not be found. The final selection consists of the twenty-one indicators, thirteen monthly and eight quarterly, listed in Tables 1, 3, 4 and 5, and shown in Appendixes A and B. All quarterly series are from the national income accounts and are interpolations in semi-annual official data, prepared and published by the German Institute for Business Cycle Research.[16]

The omission of the unemployment rate from the list of indicators deserves a word of comment since it would usually be regarded as one of the most significant series. In Germany, however, the rate remained almost

---

[16]In two instances where comprehensive measures of important activities are available only quarterly, we have supplemented them by monthly measures with narrower coverage. This goes for the national income accounts series, Investment in Equipment, which is supplemented by the component of the industrial production index, Production of Investment Goods. It goes, further, for the national accounts series, Income of Employees, supplemented by Industrial Wages and Salaries. In both instances the heavier weight given to these measures in this fashion was deemed appropriate.

constant (at a very low level) over much of the period. This is evidently due to the fact that variations in the demand for labor were absorbed by variations in the rate of immigration of foreign workers and therefore are not reflected in the unemployment rate. The number of unemployed is one of our indicators, however.

German official sources as well as the German Institute for Economic Research have only recently begun to adjust their series for seasonal variations. For the most part, they base their analyses on same-month-year-ago comparisons despite of the shortcomings of this method. The Organization for Economic Cooperation and Development (OECD) publishes some German series in seasonally adjusted form but only beginning with 1955. Thus all nineteen out of the twenty-one series which do exhibit seasonal fluctuations were adjusted at the NBER.[17]

---

[17]The adjustment is made by the X-11 Variant of the Census Method II. This seasonal adjustment program provides a "modified seasonally adjusted series" which is the one we have used in adjusting the German indicators. The modification consists in replacing the extreme values of the series with the corresponding values of a smoothed version (a Henderson curve) of the series. The method is described in Julius Shiskin, Allan H. Young and John C. Musgrave, *The X-11 Variant of the Census Method II Seasonal Adjustment Program,* Technical Paper No. 15, Bureau of the Census, February 1967.

Deviation cycles

Deviation cycles are based on the adjustment of indicators for their upward trends. Hence, they encounter the common objection to reliance on trend-adjusted series, the unavoidable arbitrariness involved in selecting the trend curve. Dates of cycle turns and even the existence of cycles depend on the definition of the trend. The objection is valid and is the reason for employing a second entirely different procedure, the identification of cycles in growth rates. Thus the results obtained with one method are checked against those obtained with the other.

The arbitrariness of the trend adjustment is also reduced, as far as possible, by applying the same formula to all twenty-one indicators. This could not have been done with fitted trends because of the diversity of long-run movements among indicators. In some instances a series' movements have shifted over time and two or more trends would have had to be fitted to a single indicator. Since it is unadvisable to fit several trends to a period of only eighteen years and even more unadvisable to adjust different indicators in different ways, we decided on using a long-term moving average which is flexible enough to cope with the diversity of trends. In order to iron out cyclical swings a term of six to seven years is required. We chose a seventy-five-month moving average as a convenient figure that fits the requirement. The missing thirty-seven months at either end of the moving average are supplied with the help of its average rate of change during the first two years and the last two years for which it is available. This method of extrapolation implies that the series proper is assumed to repeat in the period not covered by the data, its pattern during the first years and the last years which are covered by the data. The trends are shown in the top panels of Charts A-1 to A-21. The only indicators which show horizontal trends are inventory changes and short-term lending changes.[18]

The percentage deviations of the series from their moving average trends represent the deviation cycles of the indicators whose turning points are to be determined (the second panels on Charts A-1 to A-21).

The turning points have been selected by a new objective method, a computer program developed at the NBER by Gerhard Bry and Charlotte Boschan.[19]

---

[18]Even these two series have been fitted with a trend in order to measure their movements in the same fashion as those of the other indicators.

[19]Gerhard Bry and Charlotte Boschan, *Cyclical Analysis of Time Series: Selected Procedures and Computer Programs,* New York, NBER, forthcoming.

This method consists, essentially, in first identifying major cyclical swings, then delineating the neighborhoods of their maxima and minima, and finally narrowing the search for turning points to specific calendar dates. All procedures are performed on seasonally adjusted data.

This stepwise approach to the selection of turns is necessary because most time series are much too choppy for direct mechanical selection of cyclical maxima and minima. Such a procedure would, instead, give a large number of highs and lows most of which would indicate only a brief fluttering of the data rather than a cyclical turn. For this reason the existence of cycles must first be determined in a smoothed form of the series before the precise date can be selected in the unsmoothed data.

The first curve from which turning points are determined, after adjustment for extreme values, is a twelve-month moving average. This is a convenient means for eliminating fluctuations of subcyclical duration or of very shallow amplitudes. The rule for selecting turning points is: any month whose value is higher than those of the five preceding months and the five following months is regarded as the date of a tentative peak; analogously, the month whose value is lower than the five values on either side is regarded as the date of a tentative trough. These tentative turns are tested for compliance to a set of constraint rules with respect to alternation of phases and duration of phases and cycles.

The next step in the process is the determination of tentative cyclical turns on the Spencer curve of the original data. The Spencer curve is selected as the next intermediary curve because its turns tend to be closer to those of the original data than those of the twelve-month moving average.[20]

In principle, the program searches, in the neighborhood (defined as ± five months) of the turns established on the twelve-month moving average, for like turns on the Spencer curve. That is, in the neighborhood of peaks, it searches for the highest of the eleven points on the Spencer curve; in the neighborhood of troughs, for the lowest. The Spencer curve turns thus located are then subjected to several tests.

They are rejected when they are (1) less than six months from either end of the series; (2) like turns and less than fifteen months apart; and (3) like turns without an intervening opposite turn.

The accepted turns in the Spencer curve provide the basis for the next step in the search for turns in the original data. In this step the series is smoothed by a three- to six-month moving average. The exact number of months depends on the time it takes for the cyclical component to exceed the irregular component in the particular series analyzed.

---

[20]The Spencer curve is a complex fifteen-month graduation formula, a weighted moving average with the highest weights in the center and negative weights at either end. This ensures that the curve follows the data closely. It has approximately the flexibility of a five-month moving average but is much smoother.

The method of deriving turning points in this moving average is practically the same as that for the Spencer curve. The highest peaks on the moving average curve within a span of five months from the dates of the peaks on the Spencer curve are selected and, correspondingly, so are the troughs.

The last step of the procedure is to find the peak and trough values in the unsmoothed data which correspond to the short-term moving average turns previously established. This search is again analogous to the previous ones. The program establishes the highest values in the unsmoothed data within a span of ± five months from the peak in the short-term moving average curve; correspondingly, the lowest value of the unsmoothed data in the neighborhood of moving average troughs is established.[21]

Having again eliminated any turns not complying to the rules, the remaining ones are accepted as the final turning points of the series.[22]

We now turn to the deviation cycles on Charts A-1 to A-21. The first impression is that most indicators move in clear-cut cyclical swings with unmistakable turning points. There is no doubt that a cyclical process was going on in almost all types of economic activities. Sharply defined cycles of particularly large amplitudes are found in indicators for unemployment, job vacancies and stock prices. Cycles of smaller amplitude but of outstanding smoothness are characteristic of series measuring the number of employees, investment in plant and equipment, current and real GNP. At the other end of the spectrum are a few indicators whose large erratic movements obscure to some extent the cyclical ones. This holds mainly for construction and for changes in lending. Prices have been stable over some periods so that the dating of turning points is sometimes difficult.

The crucial aspect of the turning points in deviation cycles of individual indicators is, of course, their consensus in time. This will be described in a later section.

---

[21] To be more precise, the span varies between four and six months, depending on the term of the moving average.

[22] In five instances (one in each of five series) the program selects a month other than the highest or lowest one as turning point. The difference between the standings of the series in the selected and in the extreme month is less than 1 per cent in three of these cases. The reason for preferring the second highest or lowest point is its occurrence in a bank of high or low standing, in contrast to an isolated maximum or minimum.

Opinions will differ regarding the acceptance or rejection by the program of borderline cases, i.e., relatively mild cycles. Since drawing the line here is a matter of subjective judgment and since the turns selected by the program seem sensible to us, we have not attempted any modifications.

It should be noted that the computer program does not utilize directly any information on the amplitude of cycles. The only way in which amplitude plays a role is that the moving averages, especially the initial, twelve-month moving average, tend to iron out minor swings (though only if they are also brief).

Step cycles

The second approach does not deal with the indicators themselves, but with their growth rates. This has the advantage of focusing on that aspect of economic change which today attracts the greatest interest. The problem with this approach is that growth rates cannot, for our purpose, be analyzed in the same fashion as the original series. For one thing, their timing is different. Growth tends to be most rapid when it starts from a low base, i.e., shortly after the end of a period of slowdown or decline. Conversely, rates tend to be lowest shortly after the termination of a rapid-growth period.

Ample evidence can be found for this growth rate pattern. For instance, the rate of increase of U.S. gross national product in constant dollars was 60 per cent higher, on the average, in the first halves of the seven expansions (1921-38, 1949-61) than in their second halves. The rate of fall in the corresponding seven contractions was twice as large in the earlier part than in the later one.

Furthermore, the average monthly rate of change of thirty-four comprehensive American series before 1938 was more than twice as high between business cycle troughs and the first third of expansions than in later expansion stages. The average rate of decline was largest in the first half of contractions.[23]

Thus, if cycle phases were defined by growth rate peaks and troughs, they would tend to lead business cycles by one half to nearly one full phase. Expansions, for instance, would usually include only the beginning of a high-growth period, while most of this period would be included in the contraction phase. Since this would run counter to generally accepted ideas on business cycles, peaks and troughs in growth rates cannot serve to delimit cycle phases. Instead, the downturn must be defined as the end of a period of relatively high growth and the upturn as the end of a period of relatively low growth. In terms of growth rates, business cycles thus are defined as alternations of high and low rates, rather than as alternations of rising and falling rates. Growth rates are classified as high or low by comparisons of rates in three tentative successive cycle phases. The average rate during a high step must exceed the average rates during the preceding and succeeding low

---

[23]See Wesley C. Mitchell, *What Happens During Business Cycles,* New York, NBER, 1951, p. 299. For similar results regarding the rate of change of the money supply, see Phillip Cagan, *Determinants and Effects of Changes in the Stock of Money, 1875-1960,* New York, NBER, 1965, p. 271.

steps. The main difference between the two methods thus is in the definition of the average growth rate which serves as standard for distinguishing high and low rates. In deviation cycles the average rate is given by the long-run trend, in step cycles it is given by three successive cycle phases. If these three phases were seventy-five months long, i.e., if step cycles averaged fifty months in duration, the average rates of change obtained with the two methods should be similar since the long-run trend in deviation cycles is measured by a seventy-five-month moving average.

Step cycles were first analyzed by Milton Friedman and Anna Schwartz in their work on money. The timing of these cycles, they found, is in most instances the same as that of the trend adjusted series proper. The method we use is essentially a computerized version of their method.[24]

Analysis of rates of change also presents another problem, especially in monthly series. Month-to-month percentage changes are often highly jagged series with a sawtooth appearance and, at first glance, reveal neither cycles nor cyclical turns. The rate of change of industrial production in Chart A-13 is a good illustration.[25] To deal with this problem, we first find the approximate dates when a period of high growth ended and low growth began, and vice versa, on a chart showing the twelve-month moving average of the rates of change. It is noteworthy how clearly the underlying cyclical movements stand out in the smoothed rates of change on curve 4 in Charts A-1 to A-21 even for rates as choppy as those for industrial production (Chart A-13) and job vacancies (Chart A-4). Selecting the zone where a step turn occurred is thus not difficult in most instances. The exact month of the step turn is then tentatively identified by inspection of the chart of the unsmoothed rates.

At this point the computer program takes over. Each tentative cycle, i.e., each period between two like tentative step turns is broken into two parts at every intervening month. For each of these possible breaking points the variance between the average rates of change in the two parts (the step means) is computed. The breaking point that yields the largest variance is selected as the turning point. For instance, if a tentative cycle had a duration of twenty-four months, the program would test the variance between the mean rates of change for partitions into six and eighteen months, seven and seventeen months, eight and sixteen months, etc.

One reason for maximizing the variance rather than the simple difference between the step means is that the latter neglects the influence of

---

[24]The main difference between the Friedman and Schwartz method and ours is that Friedman and Schwartz used computations only in doubtful cases and otherwise decided by inspection, while we rely on computations in all instances.

[25]One reason is that independent errors of measurement in the original series introduce a negative serial correlation into rates of change.

the step length. Doubtful months would be assigned to the longer step, because this would increase the difference between step means even if the series' standing in the month in question were much closer to the average rate of the short step than to that of the long step.

If the computed turning point differs from the tentatively selected one, every analysis which used the latter must be repeated with the former. This procedure is continued until each upturn has been confirmed as the correct partition between the adjacent downturns and each downturn as the correct partition between the adjacent upturns. Each turn thus has to be confirmed by three computations. It must be valid (1) as the end of one cycle; (2) as the beginning of the next cycle and (3) as the correct partition between two adjacent turns of the opposite type.[26]

All the step turns in the twenty-one indicators have been confirmed in this manner. In the case of some quarterly indicators all tentative turns were validated at the first trial. For some very erratic series, on the other hand, up to fifty periods had to be partitioned before some five or six steps meeting the requirements could be identified.

It should be noted that this objective validation procedure eliminates most of the subjective element which adheres to the initial selection of the tentative turns. In some difficult cases a decision must be made whether to treat a given period as part of a step phase or as a separate step cycle. The computer program cannot handle this. In such rare instances, subjective judgment must be used.

----

[26]To illustrate: assume that December 1955 and January 1961 have been tentatively selected as dates of downturns in German industrial production. The computer program then divides the tentative cycle into two phases, the first one of low growth and the second one of high growth, at each intervening month. For each partition the variance is computed. Assume it is found that partition in April 1959 yields the largest variance between the two steps. (Partitions at points less than six months from the tentative turns are excluded by requiring a six-month minimum phase duration.)

Next, the computer-determined upturn in April 1959 is used together with the next tentative upturn in February 1963 in order to check whether the downturn in January 1961 (used previously for the selection of the upturn of April 1959), is the correct partition between April 1959 and February 1963. If the downturn in January 1961 is confirmed, we proceed to the checking of the following turn. If the downturn in January 1961 is rejected, however, and replaced by, say, March 1961, the first analysis must be repeated with the new date. This means that the period from December 1955 to March 1961 will be partitioned in the manner described above. This either may confirm the previously found upturn in April 1959 or may result in a different date. In the latter case the 1959 to 1963 analysis has to be repeated with the new date. And so on.

The first turns at either end of a series, obviously, cannot be confirmed in this fashion. All that can be done in order to identify the best possible turns at the ends is to experiment with several alternative dates. For each such date the maximum variance between the two following, or the two preceding, steps is computed. The alternative turn that yields the highest maximum variance is the one chosen.

17

TABLE 1

Comparison of Turning Points in Deviation Cycles (DC)
and Step Cycles (SC),
Twenty-One German Indicators, 1953-67
(number of turning points)

| Indicator | Turns Covered | | Matching Turns in DC and SC | | | |
	DC	SC	Total	Coincide Exactly	Differ by Months 1-3	4 and over
1. No. employed, mfg.	6	6	6	3	1	2
2. Man-hours, mfg.	7	7	7	4	0	3
3. No. unemployed, (inverted)	7	8	7	0	2	5
4. Job vacancies	7	8	7	4	1	2
5. GNP, current DM	7	9	7	6	0	1
6. GNP, 1954 DM	7	7	7	4	0	3
7. Investment, equipment, 1954 DM	7	7	7	5	1	1
8. Investment, constr., 1954 DM	8	10	7	7	0	0
9. Inventory changes, 1954 DM	7	9	7	7	0	0

(continued)

TABLE 1 (continued)

Indicator	Turns Covered DC	Turns Covered SC	Matching Turns in DC and SC Total	Coincide Exactly	Differ by Months 1-3	Differ by Months 4 and over
10. Employee income	6	6	6	5	0	1
11. Disposable income	9	9	9	6	1	2
12. Property and entrepreneurs' income	7	7	6	5	0	1
13. Indus. prod., total	7	7	7	4	2	1
14. Indus. prod., investment goods	7	7	7	4	0	3
15. Wages and salaries, mfg.	6	9	6	4	0	2
16. Sales, domestic, mfg.	7	9	7	6	1	0
17. Producers' prices, indus. prod.	6	7	6	4	0	2
18. Stock prices, industry	7	7	7	4	0	3
19. Short-term lending changes	8	10	7	6	0	1
20. Imports, raw materials, indus.	7	7	7	5	0	2
21. Imports of semimfgs., indus.	7	7	7	4	1	2
Total, all indicators	147	163	144	96	10	38

NOTE: Pre-1953 turns are omitted from this table. Series numbers 5 through 12 are quarterly, other series are monthly. Step cycles are cycles in growth rates, deviation cycles are cycles in percentage deviations from trends.

The steps are indicated in Charts A-1 to A-21, by horizontal lines drawn at the average level of the step. On the whole, the timing of the step cycles agrees well with that of the deviation cycles. This is shown for individual indicators in the aforementioned charts, and by a summary count for all indicators in Table 1.

The table shows that 96 out of 147 turns in deviation cycles coincide exactly with the corresponding step cycle turns. Another forty-eight turns can be classified as matching although there are intervals of one month to two years between them. Conversely, only 3 turns in deviation cycles and 19 out of 163 turns in step cycles are not matched by similar turns in the other type of cycle.

This correspondence is impressive when one considers the difference in methods used, the large erratic component of the movements analyzed and the numerous borderline cases. Most divergent turns are matters of double peaks or double troughs, with different selections made by the two types of analysis. The downturns in job vacancies, 1955-56 (Chart A-4) are an example. The deviation cycle analysis picks the later of two downturns (April 1956), the step cycle analysis the earlier (August 1955).

Another example is the 1965 downturn in industrial production. In this case it is the deviation cycle which gives the earlier and the step cycle which gives the later turn.

Clearly, agreement between the step and deviation turns is much better at certain dates than at others for most indicators. There are strong turns and weak turns, as will be brought out further in the discussion of the reference cycles. The greatest uncertainty surrounds the turns at either end of the period covered. The deviation cycles are here based on extrapolated trends which may differ widely from actual ones. Similarly the growth rate step averages cannot be compared to preceding nor to following ones. Hence turns close to the beginning or end of the series should be considered highly tentative.

We shall see below that the discrepancies which do occur between the two types of cycles in individual indicators are largely eliminated when the indicators are combined into business cycles.

Business cycles

Having determined the turning points in the deviation cycles and step cycles of each of the twenty-one indicators, the remaining task is to combine them into a business cycle chronology. This is done by a simple mechanical procedure rather than by the NBER method of selecting the reference turns for the United States. The difference in method is due to the difference between our materials and those available for the same purpose for the United States. For the U.S. we can (1) utilize numerous indicator series; (2) rely on a large stock of information, accumulated over decades, regarding the timing and regularity of these indicators; and (3) draw upon a vast body of other information on the United States economy. All these sources of knowledge are not at our command for foreign cycles.

From extensive experiments with U.S. data we are in a position to know that the mechanical procedures used are likely to yield business cycle turning dates very close (i.e., within a month or two) to those obtained by less mechanical methods. Our method relies on the count, for each month covered, of the number of indicators in expansion as defined in one instance by their deviation cycles, and in the other by their step cycles. Periods in which the majority of indicators move from upturn to downturn are speedup phases. Periods when the majority of indicators move from downturn to upturn are slowdown phases. The last month of the phase is the turning point. This can also be described as constructing a diffusion index defined as the excess of the percentage of indicators expanding over the percentage contracting in a given month. The last month before the index crosses the zero line is the turning date.[27]

---

[27] *The treatment of turns in quarterly series:* It is customary to assume that turns in quarterly series occur in the center month of the quarter. The computation of the diffusion index also rests in general on this assumption. The assumption is dropped, however, and the month of turn is determined by a more refined procedure, when a business cycle turning point occurs during an indicator's turning quarter.

Three sets of diffusion indexes are computed, placing the indicator turns into the first, second and third months, respectively. From these three indexes the final index and the final turning month are selected by the following rules.

1. When all three indexes turn in the same month, that month is selected as the quarterly indicator's turn. This has the effect that the difference between the standings of the index in the month of the turn and the subsequent month is larger than it would be if the quarterly turn had been assumed to occur in one of the other two months. A large step in the index after the turn is preferable to a small step.

2. When the three indexes indicate different turning months, we select the index that results in the largest step after the turn.

3. When the three indexes indicate different turns, but the magnitudes of the

The two diffusion indexes - one based on step cycles, the other on deviation cycles - are displayed in Chart 1. Both indexes trace smooth, sharp cycles of considerable amplitude. The business cycle turning dates (i.e., the points at which the indexes pass through the zero line) can, with one or two exceptions, be selected with confidence because there is practically no oscillation of the indexes around the zero lines.

Chart 2 presents the same findings in another shape. Here the differences between the per cent of indicators rising and the per cent falling are cumulated from month to month starting with an arbitrary 100 for January 1950. The cumulated curve will rise as long as more series are rising than falling, it begins to decline when the number falling exceeds the number rising. In contrast to Chart 1, it thus depicts the cycles in the accustomed way with the highest and lowest points as turning dates. The amplitudes of the curves reflect the scope and the duration of expansions and contractions. They are not affected, it should be noted, by the amplitudes of the indicator cycles.[28]

The most reassuring aspect of the findings is that four out of five business cycle turns, 1954-63, are the same whether they are based on trend adjusted indicators or on step cycles in the indicators' growth rates. The single discrepancy, at the downturn of 1955-56, is a matter of only one month. The agreement is not as close in the turns near either end of the period. The downturns in 1951 and 1965 differ by three and four months between deviation and step cycles; the upturn in 1967 differs by one month. Since, as explained previously, turns within about two years of the beginning and end of a series must be regarded as tentative, these discrepancies appear moderate.

---

steps following the turns are equal, we select the date of turn in the index which is closest in time to the corresponding turning month in the other type of cycle (deviation cycle or step cycle). This rule suffices to decide all such cases because there is no instance in which rules 1 and 2 fail for both types of cycle.

The turning points selected by the three rules are:

Rule No.	Deviation cycles		Step cycles	
1	April	1951	Dec.	1950
	Jan.	1954	Dec.	1955
	June	1967	Jan.	1961
			March	1966
2	March	1959	Jan.	1954
	Feb.	1963	Feb.	1963
	Dec.	1965	May	1967
3	Jan.	1959	March	1959
	Jan.	1961		

[28] All diffusion indexes mentioned in this study are of the "historical type," i.e., they are based on the turning points in the component series.

Curve C in Chart 1 will be discussed later on.

CHART 1

German Business Cycles, 1950-67, Net Per Cent in Expansion, Twenty-One Indicators

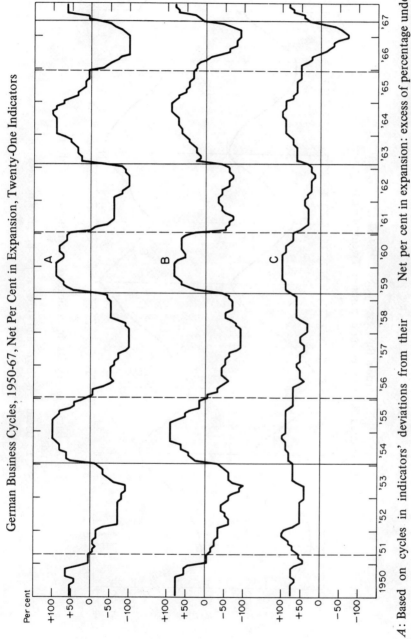

A: Based on cycles in indicators' deviations from their trends.

B: Based on high and low steps in growth rates of indicators.

C: Based on classical cycles in indicators.

Net per cent in expansion: excess of percentage undergoing cyclical expansion over percentage undergoing contraction.

Solid vertical lines indicate business cycle upturns; broken vertical lines, business cycle downturns, based on Series A.

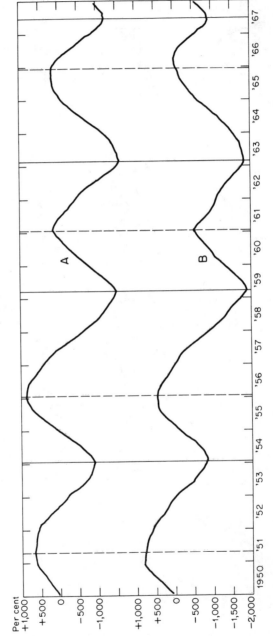

CHART 2

German Business Cycles, 1950-67,
Cumulated Net Per Cent in Expansion, Twenty-One Indicators

A: Based on cycles in indicators' deviations from their trends.

B: Based on high and low steps in growth rates of indicators. See note to Chart 1.

These findings are shown in lines 1 and 4 of Table 2. This table also allows comparison of chronologies based on subsamples of the indicators, namely, the thirteen monthly series out of the twenty-one series in the full sample. For step cycles, the turning points of the monthly series are the same as for the full sample with the single exception of a one-month discrepancy in 1965 (lines 4 and 5). For deviation cycles five turns coincide, one at either end differs slightly and the 1956 turn in the monthly series lags the full sample turn by three months. As noted previously, the date of the 1956 downturn is more uncertain than the turns in 1954, 1959, 1961 and 1963.

TABLE 2

German Business Cycle Turning Points, 1950-67;
Comparison of Results with Different Methods

	D^a	U	D	U	D	U	D^a	U^a
	\multicolumn{8}{c}{Upturn (U) or Downturn (D)}							

	D^a	U	D	U	D	U	D^a	U^a
Deviation Cycles								
1. Diffusion index (21 series)	April 1951	Jan. 1954	Jan. 1956	March 1959	Jan. 1961	Feb. 1963	Dec. 1965	June 1967
\multicolumn{9}{c}{Lend (-) or Lag (+) in Months at Turns in Line 1}								
2. Diffusion index (13 series)	- 2	0	+3	0	0	0	0	- 1
3. Modes	+10	0	+3	0	0	0	0	0
Step Cycles								
4. Diffusion index (21 series)	- 4	0	- 1	0	0	0	+3	- 1
5. Diffusion index (13 series)	- 4	0	- 1	0	0	0	+2	- 1
6. Modes	+10	0	+1	0	0	0	+5	+2

NOTE: Step cycles are cycles in growth rates. Deviation cycles are cycles in percentage deviations from trends. *Lines 1 and 4:* Eight quarterly and thirteen monthly series. *Lines 2 and 5:* Thirteen monthly series. *Lines 3 and 6:* Modes of distributions of distributions of twenty-one series.
aTentative

For another comparison, a chronology based on the modes of distributions of indicator turning points is shown in lines 3 and 6. The modes are the months when more indicators reached turning points than in any other month. The diffusion index turns are analogous to medians. The modal dates coincide with those in the full sample diffusion indexes except for the 1955-56 downturn and for the turns at the ends of the period.

In sum, by all six definitions used in Table 2, the turns in 1954, 1959, 1961 and 1963 are found in the same months. The weak downturn of 1955-56 occurs, compared to the full sample index for deviations cycles, one month earlier in the diffusion indexes for step cycles and three months later in the monthly subsample of deviation cycles. The distribution of downturns in both step and deviation cycles is bimodal in this instance with only three indicators turning in August 1955 and another three in February (step cycle) or April (deviation cycle) 1956. By contrast, from six to nine indicators turn in the months of the reference turn in 1954, 1959, 1961 and 1963.

Our aim is to present a single business cycle chronology for Germany. To work with two sets of dates, however similar to each other, would obviously be awkward and confining (see note 15). Therefore we must select either the diffusion index based on deviation cycles or the one based on step cycles or a combination of the two to be the final reference chronology. We rejected the combination because it leaves too much to subjective judgment. Of the two indexes, the one for deviation cycles was chosen since it yields cycles which are smoother and wider and thus more easily recognized than those of the step cycle index.

Smoothness can be measured by counting the months in which the diffusion index moves against the direction of the cyclical trend. Both indexes can be termed smooth by this standard. Out of 216 months covered, the step cycle index moves counter-cyclically in 24 months. Most of these are not erratic zigzag changes, but lengthy hesitations in the main cyclical forces. The most important such instance occurred from about mid-1961 to mid-1962 when the appreciation of the currency affected economic activities in differing ways.

The deviation cycle index, however, strays from its cyclical path in only 8 of the 216 months, showing a near perfect degree of smoothness.

When the index amplitude is defined as the distance traveled from its highest to its lowest point and back again, the maximum possible amplitude per cycle is 200 per cent. The actual average amplitude of the step cycle index in 3½ cycles is 176 per cent, that of the deviation cycle index is 195 per cent. In both instances the amplitudes are very high indicating that in all cycle phases there are months where nearly all series move together. The deviation cycle index reaches the possible maximum for a phase, 100 per cent, in five cycle phases. In the remaining two phases, twenty of the twenty-one series agree in some months.

The arithmetic mean of the diffusion indexes for the entire period, computed without regard to sign, also measures the consensus of the indicators. It shows that the excess of indicators moving in one direction over those moving in the opposite direction was *on the average* 55 per cent for step cycles and 60 per cent for deviation cycles. Again we find general agreement among the indicators with the deviation cycle index coming out on top.

Comparison among individual business cycle turns and among individual indicators

Having studied the average relationships one may want to learn about the variations among cycle turns and among indicators. Tables 3 and 4 tell the story.

Perhaps the most important feature brought out in these tables is the regularity with which all the indicators turn near all business cycle turns. Out of 164 comparisons there are only 7 instances in the deviation cycles and 6 in step cycles when an indicator fails to turn in the neighborhood of a business cycle turn. Even these few cases occurred almost exclusively at the two terminal turns (Table 4, column 7). The close correspondence between indicator cycles and business cycles is further reflected in the timing of the turns. About 50 per cent of all indicators turn within three months from the corresponding business turns and the average distance of all indicators from business turns is only four to five months (Table 4, column 10).

Comparison among the eight business cycle turns shows a distinct difference between upturns and downturns. Dispersion of indicator turns around upturns is smaller than around downturns. The average deviation of indicator upturns at the four business upturns is 3.7 months, that of indicator downturns at the four business downturns is 5.8 months (based on Table 3, last lines).[29]

The differences in timing among the twenty-one indicators are also of interest. Judging by the number of leads and lags and by median leads and lags at business cycle turns, we find that thirteen indicators tend to coincide roughly with business cycles. Two indicators, stock market prices and imports of semimanufactures, show a distinct tendency to lead. On the other hand, four series tend to lag: wages, personal income, disposable income and commodity prices. The irregular behaviour of the two remaining series defies generalization. Not surprisingly, these are the series depicting month-to-month changes, in inventories, and in lending respectively.

Finally, it is interesting to compare the timing of the German indicators to their counterparts in the United States. In evaluating this comparison one must keep in mind that (1) most German indicators are defined differently

---

[29] Please note that the somewhat larger average deviations of step cycles as compared to deviation cycles merely reflect our choice of deviation cycles for business cycle turns.

than the corresponding U.S. ones; (2) the time period covered differs between the two set of measures with U.S. timing measures pertaining to varying periods; (3) the cycle concepts and the methods used to set specific and reference turns differ between the German and the U.S. cycles.

In view of all this, the similarity both of the ordering and of the magnitude of median leads and lags is certainly striking (Table 5). It indicates the close relations between the two cycle concepts and dating methods.

The only series with distinctly different timing in the two economies are prices and incomes, especially wage incomes. The turns in these indicators tend to coincide with U.S. business cycle turns and to lag at German ones, whether upturns or downturns.

In part, at least, the income lag may be due to the hoarding of labor connected with the tightness of the German labor market. (This is reflected also in the small lags of the employment indicator.) Labor union policies may be another contributing factor.[30] Regarding prices, it may be noted that formerly wholesale prices lagged in the U.S. as well, particularly at upturns, and consumer prices continue to do so. A priori, one expects prices to lag and the recent coincidence in the U.S. seems to call for an explanation rather than the lag in Germany.

---

[30]I am indebted to Dr. W.H. Strigel, Director, IFO-Institut fuer Wirtschafts-forschung, for clarifying this point.

TABLE 3

Leads (-) and Lags (+), in Months, of Turns in
Twenty-One German Indicators at German Business Cycle Turns;
Deviation Cycles (DC) and Step Cycles (SC), 1950-67
(by business cycle turns)[a]

Indicators	(4)1951 Downturn	(1)1954 Upturn	(1)1956 Downturn	(3)1959 Upturn	(1)1961 Downturn	(2)1963 Upturn	(12)1965 Downturn	(6)1967 Upturn
1. No. employed, mfg.								
DC	n.a.	0	+ 3	0	+ 2	+ 9	+ 1	N
SC	n.a.	0	+ 3	+ 2	+ 2	+13	- 9	N
2. Man-hours, mfg.								
DC	0	- 8	+ 5	0	+ 2	- 2	0	- 1
SC	0	- 8	+ 5	0	-10	+18	- 9	- 1
3. No. unemployed (inverted)								
DC	n.a.	+ 7	+ 3	-11	+ 1	+10	+ 2	+2
SC	n.a.	- 3	+14	- 1	+12	- 1	+ 5	-1
4. Job vacancies								
DC	n.a.	- 1	+ 3	- 3	- 1	0	0	- 2
SC	n.a.	- 1	- 5	- 3	- 1	-19	+ 2	- 2

(continued)

TABLE 3 (continued)

Indicators	(4)1951 Downturn	(1)1954 Upturn	(1)1956 Downturn	(3)1959 Upturn	(1)1961 Downturn	(2)1963 Upturn	(12)1965 Downturn	(6)1967 Upturn
5. GNP, current DM								
DC	+10	0	+ 4	0	0	0	0	+2
SC	+10	0	+ 4	0	0	0	+ 5	+2
6. GNP, 1954 DM								
DC	- 5	0	+ 4	-10	0	0	+ 5	+2
SC	- 3	0	- 8	0	0	-18	+ 5	+2
7. Invest., equipment, 1954 DM								
DC	- 5	- 2	- 5		0	+ 3	-10	0
SC	- 4	- 2	- 5		0	+ 3	+ 3	-1
8. Investment, constr., 1954 DM								
DC	N	0	- 8	-13	0	0	-13	+2
SC	N	0	- 8	-13	0	0	N	+2
9. Inventory changes, 1954 DM								
DC	+10	- 8	- 5	0	+ 4	+ 6	- 4	-4
SC	N	+ 7	- 5	0	+ 4	+ 6	- 4	-4

(continued)

31

TABLE 3 (continued)

	(4)1951 Downturn	(1)1954 Upturn	(1)1956 Downturn	(3)1959 Upturn	(1)1961 Downturn	(2)1963 Upturn	(12)1965 Downturn	(6)1967 Upturn
10. Employee income								
DC	+10	0	+13	+ 2	+13	+ 9	- 7	N
SC	+10	+ 7	+ 1	+ 2	+13	+ 9	- 7	N
11. Disposable income								
DC	+13	+ 4	0	+14	+13	0	- 7	+2
SC	+10	+ 4	+ 1	+14	- 2	0	+ 8	+ 2
12. Property and entrepreneurs' income								
DC	+10	- 8	- 2	0	-11	0	-13	+2
SC	+19	- 8	N	0	-11	0	+11	+2
13. Industrial prod., total								
DC	0	0	- 1	+ 1	0	- 1	- 8	0
SC	- 8	+ 2	- 1	+ 1	0	- 1	+ 6	- 3
14. Industrial prod., invest. goods								
DC	- 2	- 5	- 2	+ 1	0	0	-11	0
SC	- 4	+ 7	- 6	+ 1	0	0	+ 6	0

(continued)

TABLE 3 (continued)

Indicators	(4)1951 Downturn	(1)1954 Upturn	(1)1956 Downturn	(3)1959 Upturn	(1)1961 Downturn	(2)1963 Upturn	(12)1965 Downturn	(6)1967 Upturn
15. Wages and salaries, mfg.								
DC	+ 2	+ 4	+ 7	+ 5	+16	+10	+ 3	N
SC	+ 2	+ 4	+ 1	+ 5	- 1	+10	+ 8	- 2
16. Sales, domestic, mfg.								
DC	n.a.	0	- 1	0	+ 2	0	0	- 1
SC	n.a.	0	- 1	0	- 1	0	0	- 1
17. Producers' prices, indus. prods.								
DC	+ 7	+ 8	+11	+ 4	+15	+17	+ 4	N
SC	+ 8	- 2	+11	+ 4	0	+17	+ 4	+4
18. Stock prices, industry								
DC	+ 9	- 7	- 5	-10	- 5	- 4	-15	- 5
SC	+ 9	- 7	- 9	-10	- 5	- 4	-21	+1

(continued)

TABLE 3 (continued)

Indicators	(4)1951 Downturn	(1)1954 Upturn	(1)1956 Downturn	(3)1959 Upturn	(1)1961 Downturn	(2)1963 Upturn	(12)1965 Downturn	(6)1967 Upturn
19. Short-term lending changes								
DC	N	N	- 4	-11	- 4	+ 7	+ 3	-3
SC	+ 5	-18	+17	-11	+ 6	+ 7	+ 3	-3
20. Imports, raw materials, indus.								
DC	+ 5	+ 1	+16	- 1	0	0	+ 5	-1
SC	+ 5	+ 1	+16	-10	0	0	-12	-1
21. Imports, semimfgs., indus.								
DC	- 5	- 6	- 7	- 1	-10	- 1	-11	-3
SC	- 5	0	- 9	- 1	-10	+13	-11	-3

(continued)

TABLE 3 (continued)

All Indicators	(4)1951	(1)1954	(1)1956	(3)1959	(1)1961	(2)1963	(12)1965	(6)1967
Mean Lead (-) or Lag (+)								
DC	+3.9	- 1.0	+1.4	- 1.0	+1.8	+3.0	- 3.6	- 0.5
SC	+3.3	- 0.8	+0.8	- 1.0	- 0.2	+2.5	- 0.3	- 0.4
Aver. deviation from bus. cycle turns								
DC	6.2	3.4	5.2	4.1	4.7	3.8	5.8	1.9
SC	7.1	3.9	6.5	3.7	3.7	6.6	6.9	1.9

NOTE: Series numbers 5 through 12 are quarterly, other series are monthly. Step cycles are cycles in growth rates, deviation cycles are cycles in percentage deviations from trends.

n.a. = data not available.

N = no matching turn.

[a]The numbers in parentheses refer to months, i.e., 1 is January, 4 is April, etc.

TABLE 4

Summary of Relations of Turns in Twenty-One
Indicators to German Business Cycle Turns;
Deviation Cycles (DC) and Step Cycles (SC), 1950-67

Indicator	Number of:							Average Months		
	Leads		Exact Coinci- dences	Lags		Unrelated Turns in		Lead (-) or Lag (+)		Dev. from Ref. Turn
	Long	Short		Short	Long	Indi- cator	Business Cycle	Median	Mean	
	(1)	(2)	(3)	(4)	(5)	(6)	(7)	(8)	(9)	(10)
1. No. employed, mfg.										
DC	0	0	2	3	1	0	1	+1.5	+2.5	2.5
SC	1	0	1	3	1	0	1	+2.0	+1.8	4.8
2. Man-hours, mfg.										
DC	1	2	3	1	1	0	0	0.0	-0.5	2.2
SC	3	1	2	0	2	2	0	-0.5	-0.6	6.4
3. No. unemployed (inverted)										
DC	1	0	0	4	2	0	0	+2.0	+2.0	5.1
SC	0	4	0	0	3	2	0	-1.0	+3.6	5.3
4. Job vacancies										
DC	0	4	2	1	0	0	0	-1.0	-0.6	1.4
SC	2	4	0	1	0	2	0	-2.0	-4.1	4.7

(continued)

TABLE 4 (continued)

Indicator	Number of:					Unrelated Turns in		Average Months		
	Leads		Exact Coinci- dences	Lags				Lead (-) or Lag (+)		Dev. from Ref. Turn
	Long	Short		Short	Long	Indi- cator	Business Cycle	Median	Mean	
	(1)	(2)	(3)	(4)	(5)	(6)	(7)	(8)	(9)	(10)
5. GNP, current DM										
DC	0	0	5	1	2	0	0	0.0	+2.0	2.0
SC	0	0	4	1	3	2	0	+1.0	+2.6	2.6
6. GNP, 1954 DM										
DC	2	0	3	1	2	2	0	0.0	- 0.5	3.2
SC	3	0	3	1	1	0	0	0.0	- 3.4	5.1
7. Invest., in equipment, 1954 DM										
DC	3	1	3	1	0	0	0	- 1.0	- 2.4	3.1
SC	2	2	2	2	0	0	0	- 0.5	- 0.7	2.2
8. Invest., constr., 1954 DM										
DC	3	0	3	1	0	2	1	0.0	- 4.6	5.1
SC	2	0	3	1	0	5	2	0.0	- 3.2	3.8
9. Inventory changes, 1954 DM										
DC	4	0	1	0	3	2	0	- 2.0	- 0.1	5.1
SC	3	0	1	0	3	2	1	0.0	+0.6	4.3

(continued)

TABLE 4 (continued)

Indicator	Number of:					Unrelated Turns in		Average Months		
	Leads		Exact Coinci-	Lags		Indi-cator	Business Cycle	Lead (-) or Lag (+)		Dev. from Ref. Turn
	Long	Short	dences	Short	Long			Median	Mean	
	(1)	(2)	(3)	(4)	(5)	(6)	(7)	(8)	(9)	(10)
10. Employee income										
DC	1	0	1	1	4	0	1	+9.0	+5.7	7.7
SC	1	0	0	2	4	0	1	+7.0	+5.0	7.0
11. Disposable income										
DC	1	0	2	1	4	2	0	+3.0	+4.9	6.6
SC	0	1	1	2	4	2	0	+3.0	+4.6	5.4
12. Property and entrepreneurs' income										
DC	3	1	2	1	1	0	0	-1.0	-2.7	5.7
SC	2	0	2	1	2	0	1	0.0	+1.9	7.3
13. Industrial prod., total										
DC	1	2	4	1	0	0	0	0.0	-1.1	1.4
SC	1	3	1	2	1	0	0	-0.5	-0.5	2.7
14. Industrial prod., invest. goods										
DC	2	2	3	1	0	0	0	-1.0	-2.4	2.6
SC	2	0	3	1	2	0	0	0.0	+0.5	3.0

(continued)

TABLE 4 (continued)

Indicator	Number of:					Unrelated Turns in		Average Months		
	Leads		Exact Coinci-dences	Lags		Indi-cator	Business Cycle	Lead (−) or Lag (+)		Dev. from Ref. Turn
	Long	Short		Short	Long			Median	Mean	
	(1)	(2)	(3)	(4)	(5)	(6)	(7)	(8)	(9)	(10)
15. Wages and salaries, mfg.										
DC	0	0	0	2	5	0	1	+5.0	+6.7	6.7
SC	0	2	0	2	4	2	0	+3.0	+3.4	4.1
16. Sales, domestic mfg.										
DC	0	2	4	1	0	2	0	0.0	0.0	0.6
SC	0	3	4	0	0	2	0	0.0	−0.4	0.4
17. Producers' prices, indus. products										
DC	0	0	0	0	7	1	1	+8.0	+9.4	9.4
SC	0	1	1	0	6	0	0	+4.0	+5.7	6.2
18. Stock prices, industry										
DC	7	0	0	0	1	1	0	−5.0	−5.2	7.5
SC	6	0	0	1	1	0	0	−6.0	−5.7	8.2
19. Short-term lending changes										
DC	3	1	0	1	1	3	2	−3.5	−2.0	5.3
SC	2	1	0	1	4	4	0	+4.0	+0.7	8.7

(continued)

TABLE 4 (concluded)

Indicator	Number of:					Unrelated Turns in		Average Months		
	Leads		Exact Coinci- dences	Lags				Lead (-) or Lag (+)		Dev. from Ref. Turn
	Long	Short		Short	Long	Indi- cator	Business Cycle	Median	Mean	
	(1)	(2)	(3)	(4)	(5)	(6)	(7)	(8)	(9)	(10)
20. Imports, raw materials, indus.										
DC	0	2	2	1	3	0	0	+0.5	+3.1	3.6
SC	2	1	2	1	2	0	0	0.0	-0.1	5.6
21. Imports, semimfgs., indus.										
DC	5	3	0	0	0	0	0	-5.5	-5.5	5.5
SC	4	2	1	0	1	0	0	-4.0	-3.2	6.5
All indicators										
DC	37	20	40	23	37	15	7	0.0	+0.3	4.4
SC	36	25	31	22	44	26	6	0.0	+0.4	5.0

NOTE: Long leads and lags are four months and more. Short leads and lags are one to three months.

TABLE 5

Comparison of Timing of German and U.S. Indicators at Business Cycle Turns

German Indicator (1950-67)	Comparable U.S. Indicator	Median Lead (-) or Lag (+) (months)		
		German DC	SC	U.S.
18. Stock prices, industry	19. Stock prices, 500 common stocks (1870-1967)	- 5	- 6	- 4
21. Imports of semimfgs. indus.	Imports of semimfgs. (1905-1967)	- 5	- 4	0
19. Short-term lending changes	112. Change in bank loans to business (1937-1967)	- 3	+4	- 4
9. Inventory changes, 1954 DM	21. Change in business inventories, current $ (1921-1967)	- 2	0	- 2
12. Property and entrepreneurs' income	16. Corporate profits after taxes (1938-1967)	- 1	0	- 2
4. Job vacancies	301. Nonagricultural job openings (1947-1965)	- 1	- 2	0
14. Indus. prod., investment goods	Index of production of equipment, including defense (1947-1963)	- 1	0	0

(continued)

TABLE 5 (continued)

German Indicator (1950-67)	Comparable U.S. Indicator	Median Lead (-) or Lag (+) (months)		
		German		U.S.
		DC	SC	
7. Investment, equip., 1954 DM	61. Business expenditures, new plant and equipment, current $ (1947-1967)	- 1	0	+1
8. Investment, constr., 1954 DM	Gross private domestic invesment, new constr., total, current $ (1921-1966)	0	0	- 3
6. GNP, 1954 DM	50. GNP, constant $ (1921-1967)	0	0	- 2
20. Imports, raw materials, indus.	Imports of crude materials (1905-1938)	0	0	- 2
2. Man-hours, mfg.	501. Man-hours, nonfarm (1941-1966)	0	0	- 1
5. GNP, current DM	49. GNP, current $ (1921-1965)	0	+1	0
13. Indus. prod., total	47. Indus. prod. (1919-1967)	0	0	0
16. Sales, domestic, mfg.	816. Mfg. and trade sales (1938-1967)	0	0	0
1. No. employed, mfg.	Prod. worker employment, mfg., total, BLS (1913-1964)	+1	+2	0

(continued)

TABLE 5 (concluded)

German Indicator (1950-67)	Comparable U.S. Indicator	German DC	German SC	U.S.
		Median Lead (-) or Lag (+) (months)		
3. No. unemployed (inverted)	Total unemployment, NICB, Bureau of the Census (inverted) (1929-1965)	+2	-1	0
11. Disposable income	Disposable personal income (1921-1967)	+3	+3	-1
15. Wages and salaries, mfg.	53. Wages and salaries in mining, mfg., and constr. (1929-1966)	+5	+3	0
17. Producers' prices, industrial products	55. Wholesale prices, industrial commodities (1890-1967)	+8	+4	+1
10. Employee income	Compensation of employees (1946-1967)	+9	+7	+1

SOURCE: German timing from Table 4, col. 8. U.S. timing of numbered series, from Geoffrey H. Moore and Julius Shiskin, *Indicators of Business Expansions and Contractions*, Occasional Paper 103, New York, NBER, 1967, Appendix E, col. 2. U.S. timing of unnumbered series, from NBER files.

DC = Deviation cycles.
SC = Step cycles.

Classical German business cycles

What results would have been obtained had classical business cycle analysis been applied to the German data? How many turning points would have been identified and how would their timing compare to our chronology?

Two procedures have been used to ascertain the answers to these questions. The first one consists in applying to non-trend adjusted data the methods used above to obtain the deviation cycles from trend adjusted data. This requires the determination of turning points in the twenty-one indicators proper instead of in their deviations from trend. The resulting indicator cycles are again combined into a diffusion index.

The second procedure, devised by Shiskin not previously used in this paper, derives a composite index from the month-to-month percentage changes of the individual indicators. In order to express all the series in comparable units, the rates of change are standardized before being combined. The standardization is accomplished by adjusting the rates of each series so that its average month-to-month rate,without regard to direction, is 1. The standardized month-to-month percentage changes of the twenty-one indicators are summed for each month and chained into an index with the value for the first month covered set equal to 100.[31]

The composite index is more flexible than the diffusion index (Chart 3) because it reflects monthly movements of the indicators while the diffusion index reflects phases in the indicators' cycles. A small decline occurring simultaneously in the majority of indicators may show up as a decline in the composite index but need not do so in the diffusion index because the downward movements of the indicators may not qualify as recession phases. Therefore the chance of identifying a recession is greater with the composite index than with the diffusion index.

However, in our case the composite index concurs with the diffusion index: both failed to record any classical recession in Germany, 1950-66. Despite its greater flexibility the composite index falls in only 30 of the 192 months, 1950-65. Of these thirty months, twenty-three are declines of only one or two months' duration. The only two declines of more than two

---

[31]For a detailed description of the derivation of composite indexes, see Julius Shiskin, *Signals of Recession and Recovery:An Experiment with Monthly Reporting,* Occasional Paper 77, New York, NBER, 1961, Appendix A. Also Geoffrey H. Moore and Julius Shiskin,*Indicators of Business Expansions and Contractions,* Occasional Paper 103, New York, NBER, 1967, p. 83.

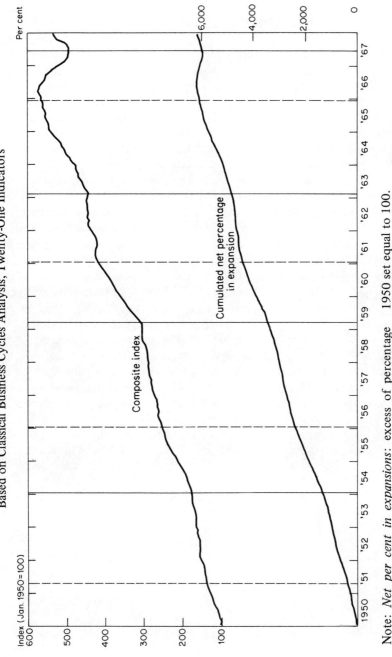

CHART 3

Course of the German Economy, 1950-67,

Based on Classical Business Cycles Analysis, Twenty-One Indicators

Note: *Net per cent in expansions*: excess of percentage undergoing cyclical expansion over percentage undergoing contraction.

Composite index: based upon average of amplitude — adjusted rates of change of twenty-one indicators with January 1950 set equal to 100.

Solid vertical lines indicate business cycle upturns; broken vertical lines, business cycle downturns, based on cycles in indicators' deviations from their trends. See Charts 1 and 2.

months (one of three months, one of four months), occurred during the 1961-63 slowdown and both were not only brief but also mild. There is, thus, no evidence of any classical recession until 1966-67.

For this one recession both indexes on Chart 3 give the same trough date, May 1967. But the peak dates vary, the composite index turns down in March 1966 and the diffusion index not until May. As expected, the peaks are later and the trough is earlier than in the trend adjusted chronology.

The absence of recessions prior to 1966 can be seen also in curve C of Chart 1. This shows movements of the diffusion index for classical cycles more or less paralleling those of the indexes for deviations and step cycles (curves A and B), but they are of smaller amplitude. A simultaneous decline of the majority of indicators does not occur until 1966.

The composite index, it should be noted, supports our turning points which in each case mark a distinct change in its slope.

Turning points in individual indicators are marked by dots on Charts A-22 to A-26. Indicators which have practically no upward trend are, of course, expected to turn at about the same time in classical, deviation and step cycles. Indicators with mild trends, or with trends during part of the period may turn at different dates in classical cycles as compared to deviation or step cycles. Those with strong trends show very few turns in classical cycles.

Altogether, in the fourteen and a half years, January 1950 to July 1964, there are only 63 turning points in the classical cycles of the twenty-one indicators as compared to 134 turns in their deviation cycles (Table 6). Nearly all classical cycle turns match deviation cycle turns and nearly half of these matching turns fall in the same month. Significantly, where there are discrepancies, downturns in classical cycles almost always lag behind those in deviation cycles; and practically all upturns in classical cycles lead those in deviation cycles.

All this agrees with our expectations regarding the relations between classical business cycles and cycles in trend adjusted data or in growth rates.

TABLE 6

*Comparison of Turning Points
in Deviation Cycles (DC) and
Classical Cycles (CC)
Twenty-One German Indicators, Jan. 1950-July 1964
(number of turning points)*

	Downturns and Upturns	Downturns	Upturns
All turns covered			
DC	134	63	71
CC	63	29	34
Matching turns, DC and CC	57	26	31
Exactly coinciding turns, DC and CC	28	11	17
Turn in CC leading turn in DC	13	1	12
Turn in CC lagging turn in DC	16	14	2

Other investigators findings on German business cycle turning dates

It is interesting to compare our results to the views of other investigators. Such views, in most instances, refer to only one particular cycle or cycle phase. Therefore, they will be quoted cycle by cycle.

First, however, we note findings covering a longer period, the Wharton Index of Capacity Utilization, 1955-67. This quarterly index is supposed to "give a good picture of the business cycles which have occurred since 1955."[32] Actually, the turns in the index agree closely with our turns. In three instances (1959, 1961 and 1963) our turning month is within the Wharton turning quarter. In the fourth instance, the Wharton index turns in the fourth quarter of 1955, while our date is January 1956. (It may be recalled that the downturn of the step cycle diffusion index came in December 1955.) A real discrepancy, however, occurs in 1965 when the Wharton downturn comes in the first quarter and ours only in December. This downturn was difficult to set because there were double peaks in a number of indicators. Industrial production - which is what the Wharton index reflects - turned in January 1965 according to deviation cycles, but in June 1966 according to step cycles. German observers also disagree on this date as will be seen below. However, they select dates between mid-1965 and mid-1966 rather than the earlier date of the Wharton index.

In the absence of other quarterly or monthly chronologies our dates may be compared to those implied in comments on the state of the German economy. The following is a tiny sample of innumerable remarks of this kind. It is meant to convey their flavor and to show where observers agree or disagree with our dating.

That three cycles in German business activity have occurred since 1954 is widely accepted. In terms of years, upturns seem to be placed most often in 1954, 1959 and 1963-64; downturns are thought to have taken place in 1955-56, 1961 and 1965 or 1966. All of our turns occur within these years. Where they are paired, as in 1955-56 and 1965-66, the step cycle turns in one year and the deviation cycle in the other. The exception is 1964 where we find no evidence indicating that the slowdown extended into this year.

---

[32]Wharton School of Finance and Commerce, *Wharton Economic Newsletter*, University of Pennsylvania, Spring 1968, pp. 11 and 15.

In some instances analysts have designated a half-year or even a quarter as a turning date. Understandably, opinions regarding such more specific dates tend to differ among experts. Monthly dates are not discussed as far as I know.[33]

1. The Business Cycle: January 1954-February 1956-March 1959

a) Speed up in 1954-55

"Last year [1954] West Germany basked in the sunshine of international prosperity. It was able to increase its GNP growth rate significantly (by almost 25 per cent) compared to the preceding year."[34]

b) Slowdown in 1956-58

"Output in Germany has been growing more slowly since 1955 . . . . The investment goods sector experienced a noticeable slackening of home demand in the second half of 1956."[35]

"Output and incomes of the West German economy experienced continuous decline of growth rates since the boom year 1955 [through 1958]."[36]

"No doubt, therefore, the present [1958] sluggishness of the production index is also due to the slackening tendencies which, as has been repeatedly shown in these columns, have for some time been apparent in a part of the economy."[37]

---

[33] Because of the tentative nature of the 1951 downturn, the following references do not cover the contraction 1951-54.

[34] "Westdeutschland stand im vergangenen Jahr auf der Sonnenseite der internationalen Konjunktur. Es konnte seine Fortschrittsrate in der Sozialproduktsentwicklung gegenueber dem Vorjahrsfortschritt . . . betraechtlich, um fast ein Viertel . . . steigern . . ." Deutsches Institut fuer Wirtschaftsforschung, *Vierteljahrshefte zur Wirtschaftsforschung,* Berlin, 1955, Erstes Heft, p. 14.

[35] Organization for European Economic Cooperation Bulletin, *Economic Conditions in the Federal Republic of Germany,* Paris, 1957, pp. 9 and 15.

[36] "Waehrend die Gueter- und Einkommensseite der westdeutschen Wirtschaft seit dem Boom-Jahr 1955 ihren Zuwachs stetig verringerte, . . ." Deutsches Institut fuer Wirtschaftsforschung, *Vierteljahrshefte zur Wirtschaftsforschung,* Berlin, 1959, Erstes Heft, p. 14.

[37] Deutsche Bundesbank, *Monthly Report,* June 1958, p. 23.

2. The Business Cycle: March 1959-January 1961-February 1963

a) Speedup in 1959-60

"The new upswing of economic activity began in the third quarter of 1958, at first stimulated mainly by an increase in construction and rising foreign demand, but more recently by restocking throughout industry and trade and by increased government expenditure."[38]

The lead of the OECD's upturn relative to ours does not signify a real contradiction. The OECD refers to leading activities which, in our terminology, precede an upturn.

"An important feature of the situation was that the culmination of the basic surplus in late 1960, coincided with a pronounced investment boom, which had already lasted a year and a half, and rapidly rising private and public consumption. The labour market was tight and the degree of utilisation of industry capacity very high. The rise of prices and wages had steepened in the second half of 1960 and the growth of productivity had slowed down. . . .Under these conditions revaluation of the DM appeared to be the most appropriate remedy. The DM was revalued by 5 per cent in early March 1961."[39]

"Economic trends in the Federal Republic during 1960, and in the [three] months of 1961 so far surveyable, were marked by a continuing upswing. With the continuance of business activity at the highest level . . ."[40]

b) Slowdown in 1962-63

"The weakening of the expansionary forces which prevailed from 1959 to 1961 has caused problems . . . . The retardation in the West German GNP shows up very clearly. In a significantly weakened state of the economy which shows a tendency for further weakening . . . "[41]

"The features of the economic situation in the Federal Republic during 1961 and the first months of 1962 continued to be full employment, a

---

[38] OECD, *The Federal Republic of Germany,* Paris, 1960, p. 6.

[39] OECD, *Economic Surveys, Germany,* Paris, December 1964.

[40] Deutsche Bundesbank, *Report for the Year 1960,* p. 9.

[41] "Die Verringerung der 1959 bis 1961 wirksamen konjunkturellen Aufschwungskraefte hat . . . Probleme aufgeworfen . . . Die Verlangsamung im Wachstum des westdeutschen Bruttosozialprodukts ist . . . sehr deutlich zum Ausdruck gekommen. In einer merklich abgeschwaechten und sich eher weiter abschwaechenden Konjunkturlage . . ." Deutsches Institut fuer Wirtschaftsforschung, *Vierteljahrshefte zur Wirtschaftsforschung,* Berlin, 1963, Erstes Heft, pp. 16, 17.

notable rise in production (although at a slower rate than in 1960) and an upward price trend. Nevertheless the course of the business cycle in that period differed in many respects from that in 1960."[42]

"The main factor in the slower expansion of overall demand in 1962 was investment."[43]

3. The Business Cycle: February 1963-December 1965-June 1967

a) Speedup in 1963-64-65

"Economic activity expanded substantially faster in the second half of 1963 than in the first half. . . . The acceleration of economic growth since autumn 1963 . . ."[44]

Our evidence regarding the February 1963 upturn is very strong. Yet, the OECD places the date into the third quarter of 1963. This discrepancy may be due to the exceptionally rigorous winter of 1963. Our procedures which eliminate extreme values may correct more for the effects of the weather than the OECD's.

"The year 1964 brought an acceleration of the cyclical expansion in the West German economy."[45]

"In the spring of 1964 . . . the economy of the Federal Republic was in the phase of an accelerating export-induced expansion."

"Measured by the rate of capacity utilization the upper turning point was reached in the first half of 1965."[46]

b) Slowdown 1966-67

The date of the latest downturn is still controversial. Some would place it as early as about mid-1965, others decide for 1966. The ambiguity of the

---

[42] Deutsche Bundesbank, *Report for the Year 1961*, p. 46.

[43] OECD, *Economic Surveys, Germany*, Paris, January 1963, p. 22.

[44] OECD, *Economic Surveys, Germany*, Paris, January 1964, p. 13; and December 1964, p. 21.

[45] "Das Jahr 1964 hat der westdeutschen Wirtschaft eine Beschleunigung der Konjunkturellen Expansion gebracht." IFO, *Wirtschaftskonjunktur*, December 1964, p. 2.

[46] "Im Fruehjahr 1964 . . . befand sich die Wirtschaft der Bundesrepublik in der Beschleunigungphase eines export-induzierten Aufschwungs."

"Die Konjunktur erreichte ihren oberen Wendepunkt—gemessen als hoechste Kapazitaetsauslastung—im ersten Halbjahr 1965." Sachverstaendigenrat zur Begutachtung der gesamtwirtschaftlichen Entwicklung, *Stabilitaet im Wachstum*, Stuttgart und Mainz, 1967/68, pp. 116, 117.

evidence is also reflected in our analysis where deviation cycles give December 1965 and step cycles March 1966 as the downturn.

An early turn was selected, for instance, by the IFO Institut. "The tapering-off period of the growth cycle which had reached its peak in 1965 continues. Like the preceding acceleration, the retardation of growth is weaker than in 1959-63."[47]

Similarly the OECD: "As the year [1965] wore on, some slackening appeared in the rate of growth of all main types of expenditure, except building. . . .Expansion of demand had begun to slow somewhat in the course of 1965. The first half of 1966 saw little further deceleration and the weakening became marked in the second half."[48]

The German Economic Institute favors the later date: "This argues against dating the downturn in 1965 and for selecting the center part of the likely turning period, i.e., the beginning of the year 1966."[49]

The difficulty of classifying the first quarter of 1966 is reflected in this description by the Federal Minister for Economic Affairs: "The prosperity in the Federal Republic was very uneven during the first quarter of 1966, with a slight preponderance of tendencies towards cooling off."[50]

Finally, regarding the end of the slowdown: "In the summer of 1967 it became obvious that domestic demand, at least so far as it came from enterprises, was beginning to rise on a broad basis. In June for the first time a nonseasonal growth of orders from the home market was recorded by all industries, not only those producing capital goods, where the reversal had already begun earlier, but also the basic and consumer goods industries. The new upswing continued, although with slight fluctuations, until the first months of 1968 surveyable as this Report goes to press."[51]

---

[47] "Die Auslaufperiode des Wachstumszyklus, der im ersten Halbjahr 1965 seinen Hoehepunkt erreicht hatte, haelt an. Wie die vorangegangene Beschleunigung, so ist auch die Verlangsamung des Wachstums nicht so stark ausgepraegt wie im Zyklus 1959-63." IFO Institut fuer Wirtschaftsforschung Muenchen, *Wirtschaftskonjunktur,* April 1966, p. 7.

[48] OECD, *Economic Surveys, Germany* December 1965, p. 6, and March 1967, p. 5.

[49] "Dies spricht dafuer, die Markierung des Wendepunktes nicht in das Jahr 1965 zu setzen, sondern in den mittleren Teil der fraglichen Strecke, also an den Jahresanfang 1966." Deutsches Institut fuer Wirtschaftsforschung, *Vierteljahrshefte zur Wirtschaftsforschung,* Berlin, 1966, Drittes Heft, p. 255.

[50] "Die Konjunktur in der Bundesrepublik war im ersten Quartal 1966 bei einem leichten Ueberwiegen der Entspannungstendenzen stark differenziert." Der Bundesminister fuer Wirtschaft, *Die Wirtschaftliche Lage,* Erstes Vierteljahr 1966, p. 1.

[51] Deutsche Bundesbank, *Report for the Year 1967,* p. 10.

Summary

In sum, observers have characterized certain more or less precisely defined periods as times of change in the pace of the German economy. The concepts and methods used in this study give precision to these notions. The result is the selection, in each instance, of one particular month in which the German economy turned from rapid to relatively slow growth or vice versa. If accepted, such firm dates will enable analysts to measure cyclical changes in the German economy in the fashion used for the United States economy and thus to obtain comparable insights.

Although one or another of the selected dates may be shifted by a month or two on further study, the chronology deserves, in my judgment, to be accepted with confidence. The business cycles marked off by the new turning points are without doubt real phenomena, not figments of statistical procedures.

The final dates chosen are the four downturns in April 1951, January 1956, January 1961, December 1965, and the four upturns in January 1954, March 1959, February 1963 and June 1967. In a period of sixteen years we thus recognize three and a half business cycles with average durations of fifty-four and fifty-nine months for the three upturn-to-upturn and the three downturn-to-downturn cycles respectively. Compared to United States classical business cycles, 1945-61, which ran on the average for forty-six months, our German cycles are somewhat longer. They are shorter, on the other hand, than earlier (1879-1932) German classical business cycles which had an average duration of sixty-four months.[52]

As expected, the durations of the cycle phases differ far more between trend adjusted cycles and classical cycles than the durations of entire cycles. Defining cycle phases as periods of below and above average growth tends to make their average lengths somewhat similar. When, on the contrary, expansions and contractions are defined as absolute rises and declines and upward trends predominate, expansions will be much longer than contractions. Thus, classical German expansions (1879-1932) lasted thirty-seven months on the average and contractions twenty-seven months. The duration of U.S. classical expansions, 1945-61, averaged thirty-six months and that of contractions only eleven months.

It would be interesting, of course, to compare the postwar course of German and United States business cycles. However, this has to await

---

[52] Burns and Mitchell, *Measuring Business Cycles,* p. 371.

identification of turning points in U.S. trend adjusted data. Without this information one cannot tell to what extent the dissimilarity between the two chronologies is due to the difference in cycle concepts and to what extent to a truly different course of the two economies.

Appendix A

1. Solid vertical lines indicate business cycle upturns; broken vertical lines, business cycle downturns.

2. In Charts A-1 to A-21, dots on curve 2 identify deviation cycle turning points.

3. In Charts A-1 to A-21, horizontal lines drawn through curve 3 indicate average rates of change during step phases. The last point of these lines is the step turn.

4. In Charts A-22 to A-26, dots identify classical cycle turning points.

5. "Manufacturing" includes mining. "Industry" includes manufacturing, mining and energy.

6. In a few instances the turning points are not maxima or minima because the highest or lowest point in a cluster of high or low points was preferred to an isolated slightly higher or lower point.

7. The slight oscillations of some curves in the charts are attributable to the fact that the computer plotting equipment plots a sloping line in small horizontal and vertical steps.

CHART A-1
Cycles in Number Employed, Manufacturing
(millions monthly)

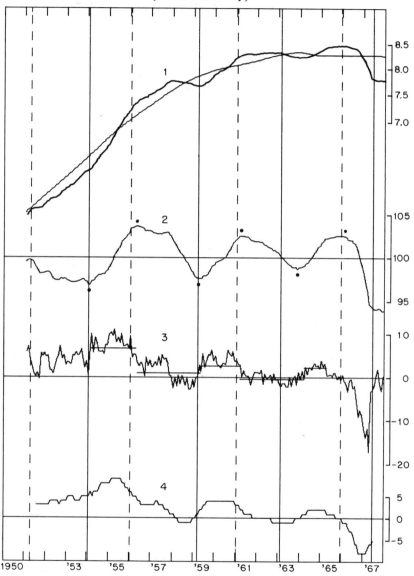

1: Seasonally adjusted data and seventy-five-month moving average.
2: Deviations from seventy-five-month moving average, per cent.
3: Change from month to month, per cent, annual rate.
4: Centered twelve-month moving average of line 3, per cent.

CHART A-2

Cycles in Man-Hours, Manufacturing
(billions monthly)

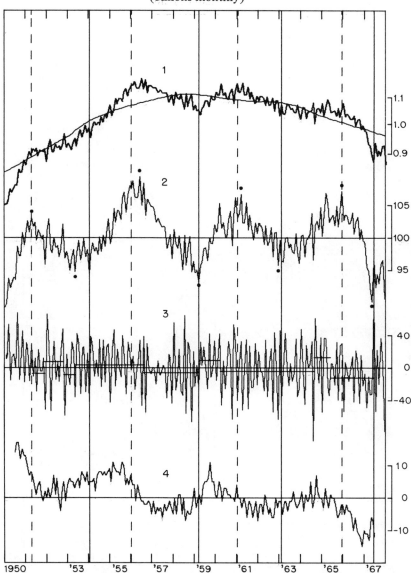

1: Seasonally adjusted data and seventy-five-month moving average.
2: Deviations from seventy-five-month moving average, per cent.
3: Change from month to month, per cent, annual rate.
4: Centered twelve-month moving average of line 3, per cent.

CHART A-3

Cycles in Number Unemployed
(thousands monthly)

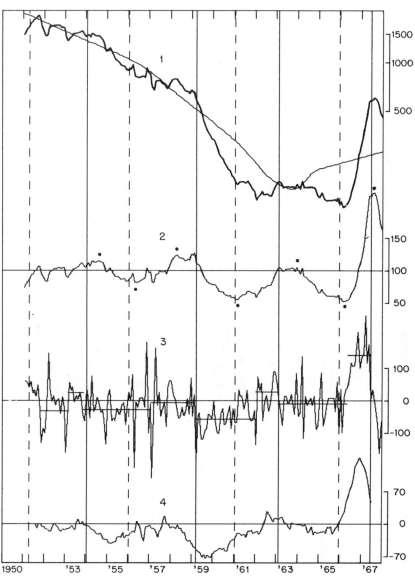

1: Seasonally adjusted data and seventy-five-month moving average.
2: Deviations from seventy-five-month moving average, per cent.
3: Change from month to month, per cent, annual rate.
4: Centered twelve-month moving average of line 3, per cent.

CHART A-4

Cycles in Job Vacancies
(thousands monthly)

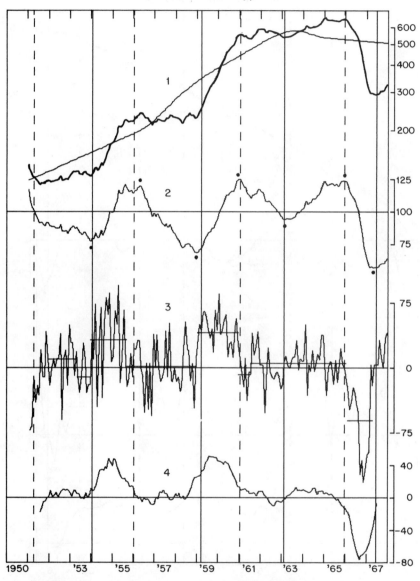

1: Seasonally adjusted data and seventy-five-month moving average.
2: Deviations from seventy-five-month moving average, per cent.
3: Change from month to month, per cent, annual rate.
4: Centered twelve-month moving average of line 3, per cent.

CHART A-5
Cycles in GNP in Billions of Current DM
(quarterly, annual rate)

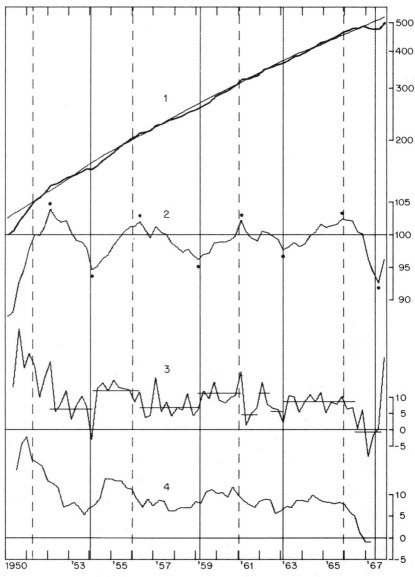

1: Seasonally adjusted data and twenty-five-quarter moving average.
2: Deviations from twenty-five-quarter moving average, per cent.
3: Change from quarter to quarter, per cent, annual rate.
4: Centered four-quarter moving average of line 3, per cent.

CHART A-6
Cycles in GNP in Billions of 1954 DM
(quarterly, annual rate)

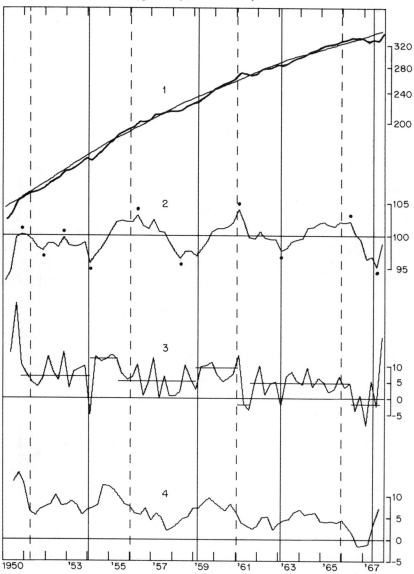

1: Seasonally adjusted data and twenty-five-quarter moving average.
2: Deviations from twenty-five-quarter moving average, per cent.
3: Change from quarter to quarter, per cent, annual rate.
4: Centered four-quarter moving average of line 3, per cent.

CHART A-7
Cycles in Investment in Equipment in Billions of 1954 DM
(quarterly, annual rate)

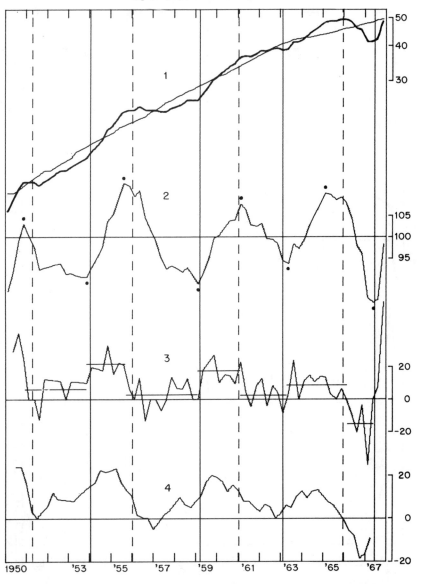

1: Seasonally adjusted data and twenty-five-quarter moving average.
2: Deviations from twenty-five-quarter moving average, per cent.
3: Change from quarter to quarter, per cent, annual rate.
4: Centered four-quarter moving average of line 3, per cent.

CHART A-8

Cycles in Investment in Construction in Billions of 1954 DM

(quarterly, annual rate)

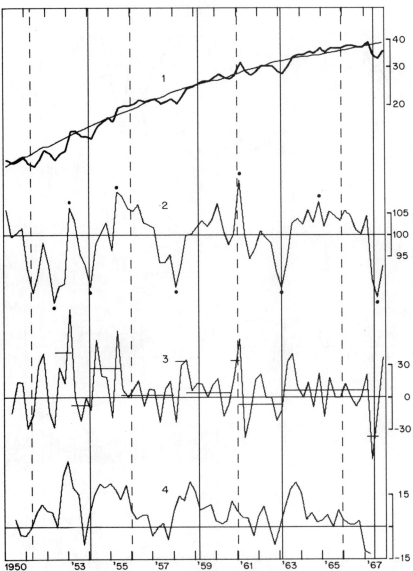

1: Seasonally adjusted data and twenty-five-quarter moving average.
2: Deviations from twenty-five-quarter moving average, per cent.
3: Change from quarter to quarter, per cent, annual rate.
4: Centered four-quarter moving average of line 3, per cent.

CHART A-9
Cycles in Inventory Changes in Billions of 1954 DM
(quarterly, annual rate)

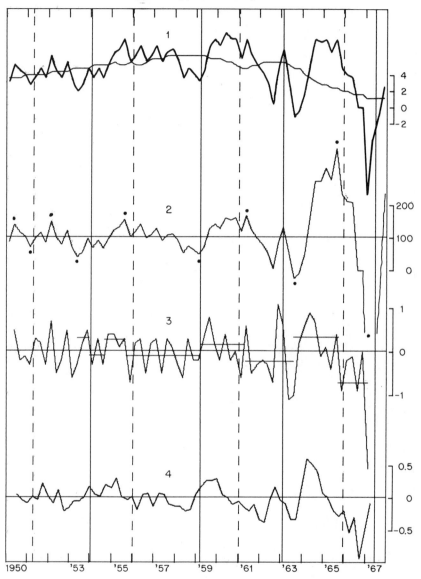

1: Seasonally adjusted data and twenty-five-quarter moving average.
2: Deviations from twenty-five-quarter moving average, per cent.
3: Change from quarter to quarter, 100 million DM, annual rate.
4: Centered four-quarter moving average of line 3.

CHART A-10
Cycles in Employee Income
(billions DM, quarterly, annual rate)

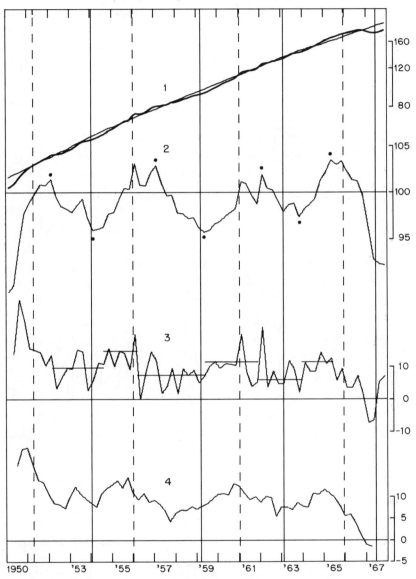

1: Seasonally adjusted data and twenty-five-quarter moving average.
2: Deviations from twenty-five-quarter moving average, per cent.
3: Change from quarter to quarter, per cent, annual rate.
4: Centered four-quarter moving average of line 3, per cent.

CHART A-11
Disposable Income
(billions DM, quarterly, annual rate)

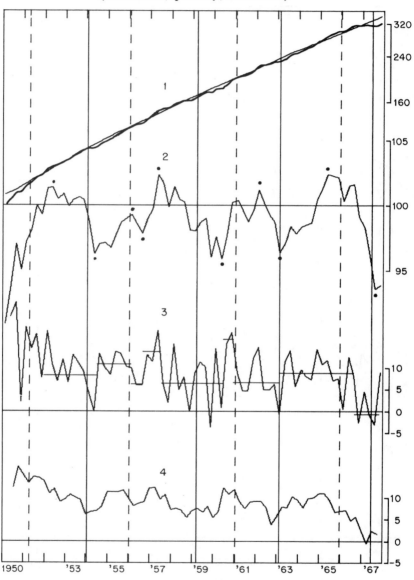

1: Seasonally adjusted data and twenty-five-quarter moving average.
2: Deviations from twenty-five-quarter moving average, per cent.
3: Change from quarter to quarter, per cent, annual rate.
4: Centered four-quarter moving average of line 3, per cent.

CHART A-12
Cycles in Property and Entrepreneurs' Income
(billions DM, quarterly, annual rate)

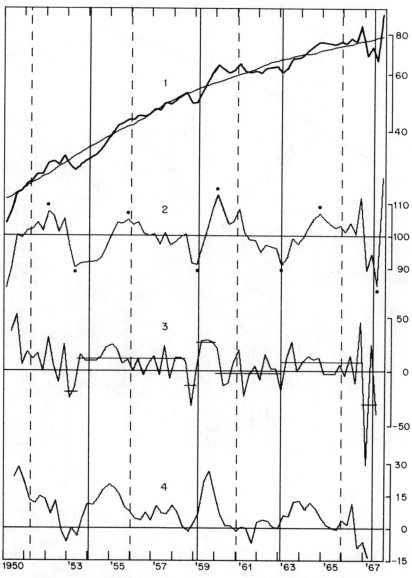

1: Seasonally adjusted data and twenty-five-quarter moving average.
2: Deviations from twenty-five-quarter moving average, per cent.
3: Change from quarter to quarter, per cent, annual rate.
4: Centered four-quarter moving average of line 3, per cent.

CHART A-13
Cycles in Industrial Production, Total
(monthly, 1960=100)

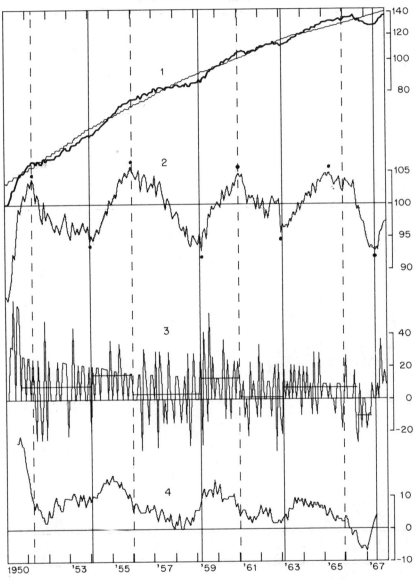

1: Seasonally adjusted data and seventy-five-month moving average.
2: Deviations from seventy-five-month moving average, per cent.
3: Change from month to month, per cent, annual rate.
4: Centered twelve-month moving average of line 3, per cent.

CHART A-14
Cycles in Industrial Production, Investment Goods
(monthly, 1960=100)

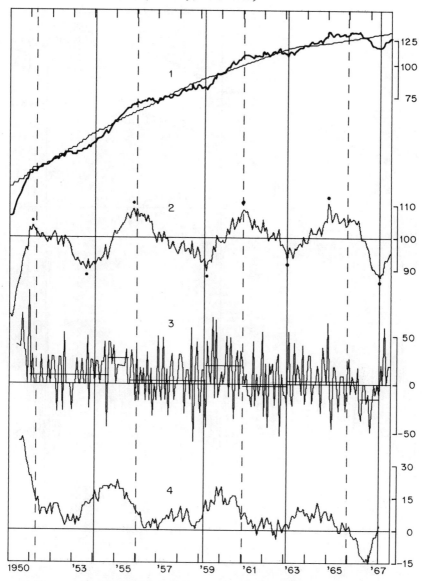

1: Seasonally adjusted data and seventy-five-month moving average.
2: Deviations from seventy-five-month moving average, per cent.
3: Change from month to month, per cent, annual rate.
4: Centered twelve-month moving average of line 3, per cent.

CHART A-15
Cycles in Wages and Salaries, Manufacturing
(monthly, billions DM)

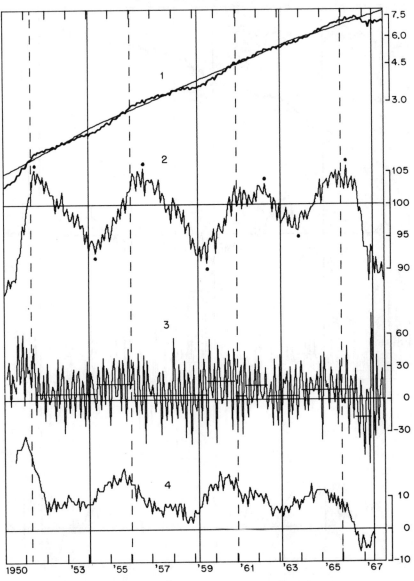

1: Seasonally adjusted data and seventy-five-month moving average.
2: Deviations from seventy-five-month moving average, per cent.
3: Change from month to month, per cent, annual rate.
4: Centered twelve-month moving average of line 3, per cent.

CHART A-16
Cycles in Sales, Domestic, Manufacturing
(monthly, billions DM)

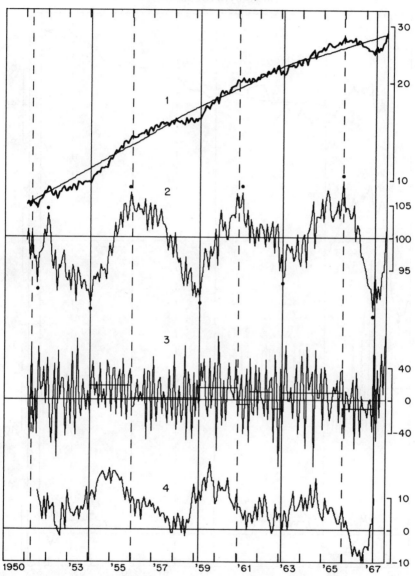

1950 '53 '55 '57 '59 '61 '63 '65 '67

1: Seasonally adjusted data and seventy-five-month moving average.
2: Deviations from seventy-five-month moving average, per cent.
3: Change from month to month, per cent, annual rate.
4: Centered twelve-month moving average of line 3, per cent.

CHART A-17
Cycles in Producers' Prices, Industrial Products
(monthly, 1962=100)

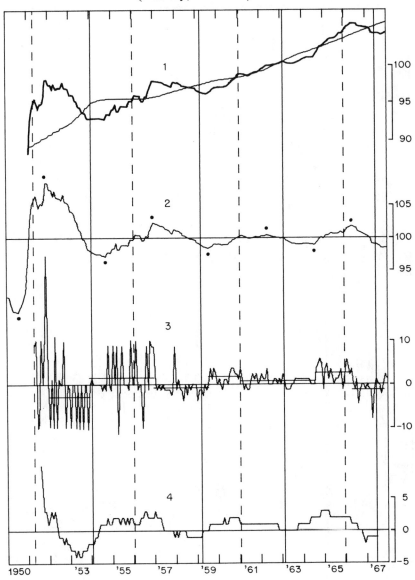

1: Original data and seventy-five-month moving average.
2: Deviations from seventy-five-month moving average, per cent.
3: Change from month to month, per cent, annual rate.
4: Centered twelve-month moving average of line 3, per cent.

CHART A-18
Cycles in Stock Prices, Industry
(monthly, 1960=100)

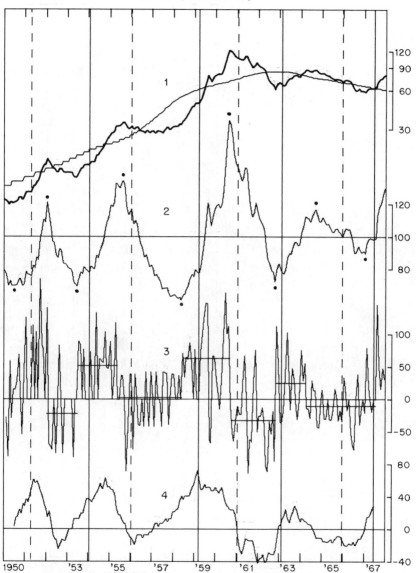

1: Original data and seventy-five month moving average.
2: Deviations from seventy-five months moving average, per cent.
3: Change from month to month, per cent, annual data.
4: Centered twelve-month moving average of line 3, per cent.

CHART A-19
Cycles in Short-Term Lending, Month to Month Changes
(millions DM)

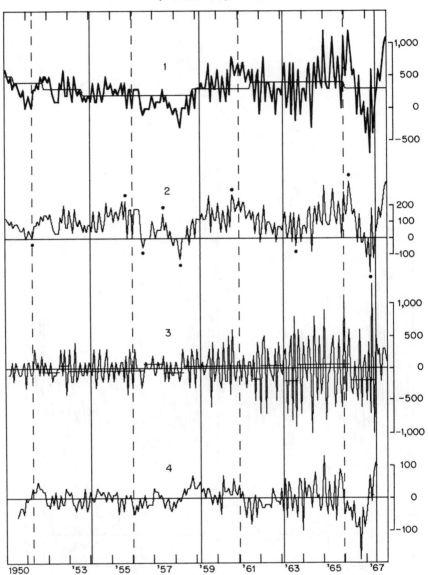

1: Seasonally adjusted data and seventy-five-month moving average.
2: Deviations from seventy-five-month moving average, per cent.
3: Change from month to month, millions DM.
4: Centered twelve-month moving average of line 3.

CHART A-20
Cycles in Imports of Raw Materials, Industrial
(monthly, millions DM)

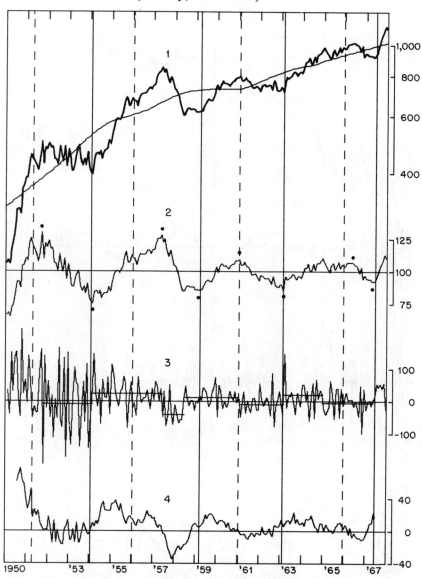

1: Seasonally adjusted data and seventy-five-month moving average.
2: Deviations from seventy-five-month moving average, per cent.
3: Change from month to month, per cent, annual rate.
4: Centered twelve-month moving average of line 3, per cent.

CHART A-21
Cycles in Imports of Semimanufactures, Industrial
(monthly, millions DM)

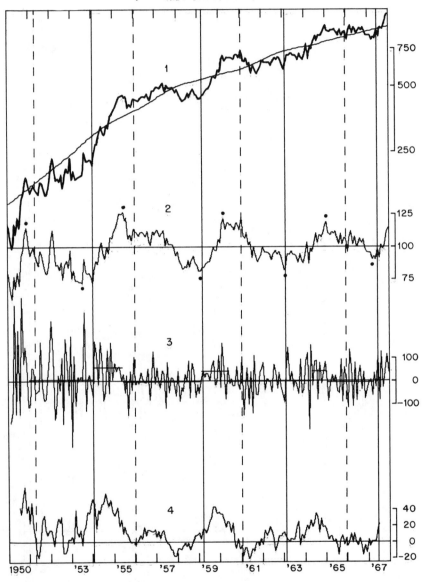

1: Seasonally adjusted data and seventy-five-month moving average.
2: Deviations from seventy-five-month moving average, per cent.
3: Change from month to month, per cent, annual rate.
4: Centered twelve-month moving average of line 3, per cent.

CHART A-22
Basic Monthly Data, Seasonally Adjusted

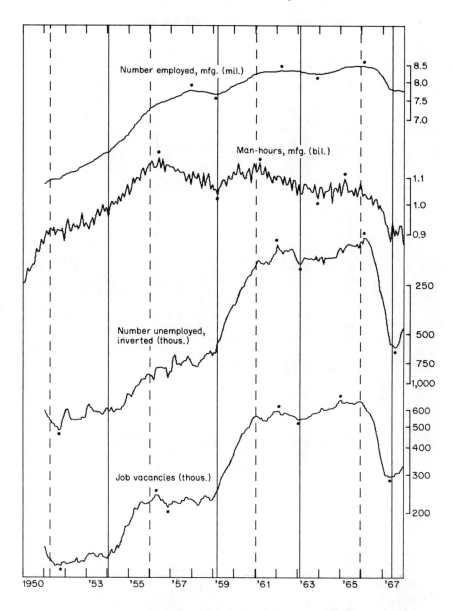

Number employed, mfg. (mil.)

8.5
8.0
7.5
7.0

Man-hours, mfg. (bil.)

1.1
1.0
0.9

Number unemployed,
inverted (thous.)

250
500
750
1,000

Job vacancies (thous.)

600
500
400
300
200

1950   '53   '55   '57   '59   '61   '63   '65   '67

CHART A-23

Basic Quarterly Data, Seasonally Adjusted

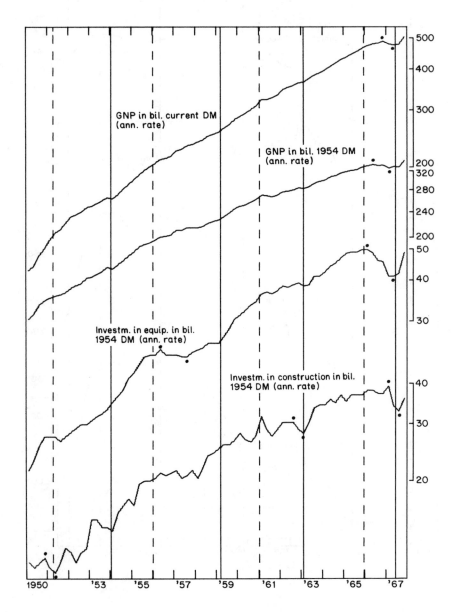

CHART A-24

Basic Quarterly Data, Seasonally adjusted

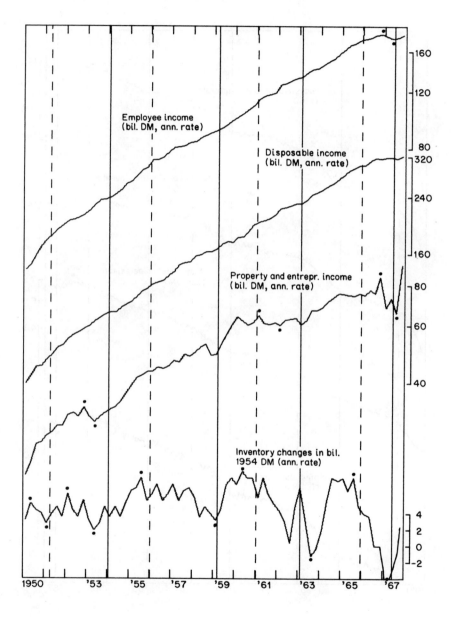

CHART A-25

Basic Monthly Data, Seasonally Adjusted

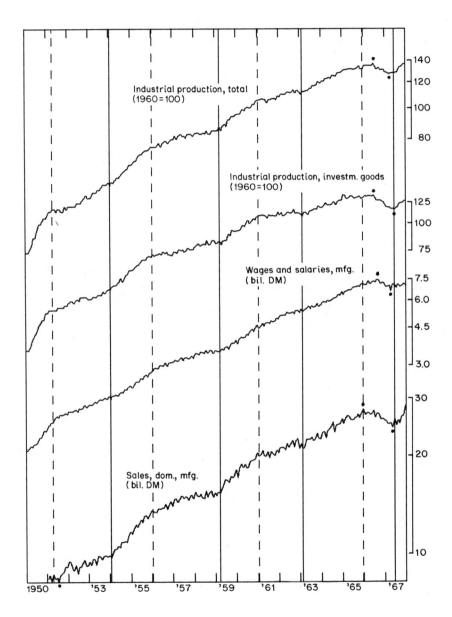

CHART A-26

Basic Monthly Data, Seasonally Adjusted

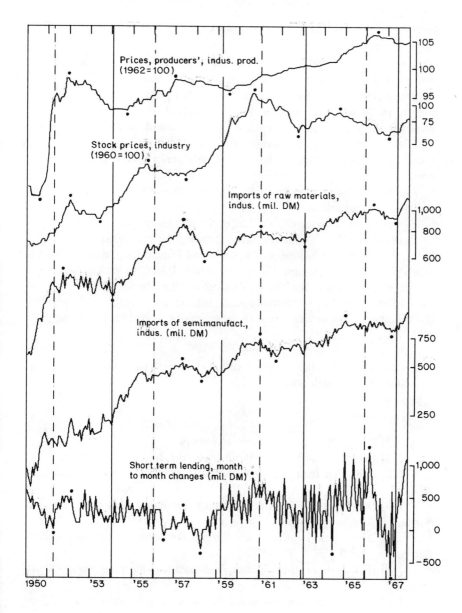

Appendix B

Basic Data Tables and Sources of German Indicators

1. General Note

This appendix presents the basic data on which the analysis of the study is based and which are shown in the charts of Appendix A.

Seasonally adjusted data are given for the full period covered for eighteen indicators. In addition, original data (i.e., before seasonal adjustment) are given for one year in order to facilitate identification of the series.

For two indicators (producers' prices and stock prices), which do not require seasonal adjustment, the original data are given for the full period covered.

For one indicator (change in lending) the data are being revised and are not given for this reason.

Figures in brackets refer to the List of Sources given below.

Saarland and West Berlin are included during the full period covered in all indicators except the following: 13. Industrial Production, Total; 14. Industrial Production, Investment Goods; 18. Stock Prices. In indicator 17. Producers' Prices, Saarland is excluded 1950-59 and West Berlin 1950-60.

"Industry" includes manufacturing, mining and energy and excludes construction. However, in series 18. construction is included and energy is excluded except in 1967.

"Manufacturing" includes mining.

Periods given in terms of years cover January through December or the first through the fourth quarter.

2. General Sources

[1] Deutsche Bundesbank, *Monthly Report*, Frankfurt am Main.

[2] Deutsches Institut fuer Wirtschaftsforschung, *Unpublished Tables*, Berlin.

[3] Deutsches Institut fuer Wirtschaftsforschung, *Vierteljahrshefte zur Wirtschaftsforschung*, Berlin.

[4] Deutsches Institut fuer Wirtschaftsforschung, *Wochenbericht*, Berlin.

[5] IFO Institut fuer Wirtschaftsforschung, *Wirtschaftskonjunktur*, Munich.

[6] Organization for European Economic Cooperation, *General Statistics*, Paris.

[7] Organization for Economic Cooperation and Development, *Historical Statistics*, Paris.

[8] Organization for Economic Cooperation and Development, *Main Economic Indicators*, Paris.

[9] Statistisches Bundesamt, *Der Aussenhandel, der Bundesrepublik Deutschland*, Wiesbaden.

[10] Statistisches Bundesamt, *Wirtschaft und Statistik*, Wiesbaden.

[11] Statistisches Bundesamt, *Statistisches Jahrbuch fuer die Bundesrepublik Deutschland*, Wiesbaden.

[12] Statistisches Landesamt, Berlin, *Statistisches Jahrbuch: Berlin*, Berlin (1951 ed. called "Berlin in Zahlen").

[13] Statistisches Amt des Saarlandes, *Saarlaendische Bevoelkerungs- und Wirtschaftszahlen*, Saarbruecken.

TABLE B1

Number Employed, Manufacturing [*Beschaeftigte in der Industrie*]
(Monthly, Thousands)

	JAN	FEB	MAR	APR	MAY	JUN	JUL	AUG	SEP	OCT	NOV	DEC
SEASONALLY ADJUSTED												
1951	5,517	5,558	5,595	5,615	5,627	5,632	5,634	5,640	5,636	5,664	5,686	5,713
1952	5,735	5,759	5,767	5,775	5,778	5,789	5,811	5,835	5,870	5,892	5,918	5,933
1953	5,956	5,969	5,982	6,007	6,033	6,061	6,090	6,115	6,149	6,173	6,184	6,203
1954	6,212	6,235	6,290	6,320	6,369	6,410	6,443	6,477	6,509	6,538	6,579	6,620
1955	6,681	6,740	6,797	6,860	6,909	6,960	7,006	7,067	7,110	7,154	7,199	7,239
1956	7,300	7,327	7,338	7,391	7,415	7,427	7,449	7,464	7,467	7,495	7,514	7,538
1957	7,551	7,559	7,579	7,599	7,624	7,656	7,630	7,719	7,747	7,770	7,774	7,775
1958	7,761	7,759	7,752	7,755	7,747	7,745	7,740	7,732	7,730	7,711	7,697	7,695
1959	7,679	7,678	7,684	7,703	7,712	7,742	7,756	7,782	7,814	7,849	7,887	7,912
1960	7,944	7,966	7,986	8,002	8,025	8,043	8,054	8,111	8,145	8,179	8,224	8,250
1961	8,277	8,297	8,316	8,317	8,329	8,331	8,331	8,319	8,305	8,314	8,314	8,322
1962	8,347	8,355	8,346	8,338	8,342	8,339	8,338	8,344	8,331	8,333	8,333	8,332
1963	8,318	8,304	8,296	8,290	8,274	8,257	8,254	8,240	8,235	8,238	8,229	8,235
1964	8,241	8,252	8,252	8,274	8,276	8,287	8,296	8,308	8,328	8,348	8,373	8,386
1965	8,404	8,426	8,454	8,469	8,471	8,471	8,456	8,465	8,466	8,464	8,473	8,466
1966	8,480	8,478	8,474	8,452	8,453	8,444	8,416	8,389	8,345	8,283	8,220	8,172
1967	8,107	8,024	7,949	7,888	7,836	7,795	7,772	7,766	7,774	7,766	7,754	7,751
ORIGINAL DATA												
1966	8,414	8,419	8,429	8,474	8,461	8,443	8,430	8,426	8,387	8,325	8,262	8,147

Source: 1951-59: data are the sum of data for the Federal Republic and for West Berlin, both from [10]. They are adjusted for the inclusion of the Saarland by data from [11, 1959 and 1961 issues].
1960-61: data are the sum of data for the Federal Republic including Saarland and for West Berlin, both from [10].
1962-63: data including West Berlin and Saarland from [11].
1964-67: data including West Berlin and Saarland from [10].

TABLE B2

Man-Hours, Manufacturing [*Arbeiterstunden in der Industrie*]
(Monthly, Millions)

	JAN	FEB	MAR	APR	MAY	JUN	JUL	AUG	SEP	OCT	NOV	DEC
SEASONALLY ADJUSTED												
1950	748	755	793	782	789	801	824	848	839	841	876	862
1951	887	901	890	912	904	914	834	910	906	903	913	874
1952	924	944	904	901	928	917	917	910	926	962	918	931
1953	926	910	935	950	922	956	977	953	973	994	969	987
1954	953	983	1,006	997	1,006	997	1,027	1,010	1,036	1,021	1,043	1,070
1955	1,034	1,053	1,096	1,076	1,096	1,097	1,086	1,123	1,138	1,107	1,138	1,153
1956	1,150	1,165	1,140	1,139	1,146	1,180	1,134	1,172	1,121	1,151	1,149	1,140
1957	1,141	1,141	1,119	1,129	1,122	1,118	1,121	1,121	1,086	1,106	1,112	1,072
1958	1,124	1,099	1,093	1,115	1,088	1,060	1,119	1,068	1,098	1,125	1,056	1,075
1959	1,056	1,058	1,037	1,065	1,069	1,089	1,030	1,066	1,104	1,112	1,094	1,124
1960	1,113	1,116	1,155	1,112	1,121	1,096	1,033	1,124	1,137	1,101	1,130	1,160
1961	1,125	1,131	1,161	1,115	1,111	1,146	1,037	1,122	1,099	1,107	1,109	1,087
1962	1,104	1,102	1,096	1,070	1,102	1,069	1,073	1,097	1,048	1,019	1,091	1,031
1963	1,071	1,038	1,031	1,074	1,074	1,054	1,059	1,046	1,040	1,096	1,041	1,018
1964	1,059	1,062	1,017	1,046	1,049	1,052	1,082	1,004	1,056	1,074	1,042	1,075
1965	1,025	1,062	1,084	1,079	1,054	1,047	1,053	1,034	1,060	1,031	1,043	1,073
1966	1,027	1,039	1,077	1,029	1,038	1,028	1,023	1,017	1,018	981	984	976
1967	972	937	913	911	894	932	904	913	896	922	915	868
ORIGINAL DATA												
1966	1,023	988	1,098	1,021	1,028	1,025	991	977	1,044	1,031	1,026	980

Source: 1950-61: data are the sum of data for the Federal Republic and for West Berlin, both from [10]. Data for 1950-58 are adjusted for the inclusion of the Saarland by data from [11, 1961 issue].
1962-63: data including West Berlin and Saarland from [11].
1964-67: data including West Berlin and Saarland from [10].

TABLE B3

Number Unemployed, Total Registered [*Arbeitslose, Insgesamt*]
(Monthly, Thousands)

	JAN	FEB	MAR	APR	MAY	JUN	JUL	AUG	SEP	OCT	NOV	DEC
SEASONALLY ADJUSTED												
1951	1,576	1,633	1,697	1,750	1,819	1,855	1,918	1,943	1,994	1,950	1,769	1,629
1952	1,542	1,640	1,694	1,744	1,753	1,779	1,750	1,761	1,768	1,663	1,706	1,663
1953	1,465	1,350	1,459	1,506	1,557	1,553	1,571	1,581	1,599	1,606	1,539	1,425
1954	1,474	1,450	1,429	1,513	1,483	1,464	1,474	1,467	1,427	1,391	1,321	1,149
1955	1,219	1,233	1,165	1,099	1,035	1,011	977	944	935	932	883	883
1956	903	903	983	812	806	791	798	805	808	794	925	852
1957	783	702	682	768	758	774	745	729	727	681	703	746
1958	787	795	798	780	746	717	704	678	658	662	637	675
1959	650	662	572	545	529	479	434	402	375	362	348	332
1960	335	317	292	267	258	254	238	226	219	216	201	197
1961	186	176	180	183	185	180	181	186	179	170	162	158
1962	141	150	154	161	153	153	155	151	150	153	165	177
1963	184	185	181	169	171	172	172	171	174	172	166	178
1964	171	166	170	169	171	169	159	170	168	170	158	148
1965	147	158	148	142	140	141	142	143	144	140	147	135
1966	140	128	129	133	138	147	152	177	194	223	266	289
1967	324	364	455	500	578	580	597	603	589	555	486	463
ORIGINAL DATA												
1966	269	236	141	121	108	101	132	106	113	146	216	372

Source: 1951-54: data are the sum of data for the Federal Republic and for West Berlin, both from [10], and for the Saarland from [13]. *January 1955-September 1965:* data including West Berlin and Saarland from [7]. *October 1965-December 1967:* data including West Berlin and Saarland from [8].

TABLE B4

Job Vacancies, Total [*Offene Stellen, Insgesamt*]
(Monthly, Thousands)

	JAN	FEB	MAR	APR	MAY	JUN	JUL	AUG	SEP	OCT	NOV	DEC
SEASONALLY ADJUSTED												
1951	138	132	122	123	120	118	115	116	115	115	118	120
1952	119	117	117	118	120	120	124	119	120	121	119	124
1953	127	133	129	131	130	126	125	129	130	127	124	123
1954	128	128	136	131	134	142	133	143	153	163	174	175
1955	176	186	194	211	207	209	221	225	221	219	222	220
1956	224	228	234	241	240	239	228	229	220	221	211	217
1957	219	226	225	223	220	221	228	226	236	233	230	230
1958	227	225	220	216	220	230	234	238	235	236	227	229
1959	234	244	253	267	282	296	307	316	328	332	352	364
1960	392	405	420	440	463	468	479	491	496	516	541	553
1961	558	555	545	550	533	531	528	546	553	565	585	587
1962	589	590	565	566	577	575	570	564	561	559	554	543
1963	535	538	544	545	545	549	555	561	576	575	580	584
1964	588	613	597	599	597	607	605	607	615	620	640	660
1965	662	645	646	650	651	641	645	637	640	652	654	654
1966	646	634	609	589	578	564	545	522	471	431	386	350
1967	322	297	298	293	294	295	296	304	307	307	316	327
ORIGINAL DATA												
1966	548	592	622	596	608	621	619	594	536	436	319	252

Source: 1951-54: data are the sum of data for the Federal Republic from [10], for West Berlin from [12] and for the Saarland from [13].
January 1955-September 1965: data including West Berlin and Saarland from [7].
October 1965-December 1967: data including West Berlin and Saarland from [8].

TABLE B5

Gross National Product in Current Deutsche Mark [*Bruttosozialprodukt*]
(Quarterly, Billions Deutsche Mark)

	1ST QUARTER	2ND QUARTER	3RD QUARTER	4TH QUARTER
SEASONALLY ADJUSTED				
1950	24.0	24.8	26.8	28.1
1951	29.8	31.3	32.1	33.4
1952	35.2	35.7	36.4	37.5
1953	37.8	38.5	39.5	40.2
1954	39.9	41.2	42.7	44.0
1955	45.7	47.2	48.7	50.2
1956	51.3	52.8	53.3	53.9
1957	56.1	56.9	58.1	58.7
1958	59.7	60.6	62.3	63.0
1959	64.0	65.9	67.5	70.0
1960	71.6	73.1	74.9	76.9
1961	80.4	80.7	81.7	83.1
1962	86.2	87.9	89.3	90.7
1963	91.2	93.6	96.0	97.3
1964	99.4	102.1	104.3	107.3
1965	108.7	111.0	113.2	116.1
1966	118.0	120.0	120.1	121.9
1967	119.4	118.9	119.0	125.8
ORIGINAL DATA				
1966	110.8	118.8	121.1	129.6

Source: 1950-59: data for the Federal Republic from [2] are adjusted for the inclusion of West Berlin and the Saarland from [2].
1960-65: data including West Berlin and Saarland from [2].
First Quarter 1966: data including West Berlin and Saarland from [3, Viertes Heft 1967].
Second Quarter 1966-Fourth Quarter 1967: data including West Berlin and Saarland from [3, Erstes Heft 1968].

TABLE B6

Gross National Product, in Constant Deutsche Mark
[*Bruttosozialprodukt, Volumen, Preisbasis 1954=100*]
(Quarterly, Billions 1954 Deutsche Mark)

	1ST QUARTER	2ND QUARTER	3RD QUARTER	4TH QUARTER
SEASONALLY ADJUSTED				
1950	28.0	29.0	31.2	32.0
1951	32.6	33.0	33.3	33.8
1952	34.9	35.6	36.1	37.4
1953	37.7	38.5	39.4	40.4
1954	39.9	41.2	42.4	43.7
1955	45.2	46.6	47.5	48.2
1956	49.0	50.3	50.4	51.0
1957	52.6	52.6	53.5	53.6
1958	53.7	54.0	55.4	56.2
1959	56.6	58.0	59.5	61.2
1960	62.3	63.1	64.1	65.3
1961	67.5	67.2	66.6	67.4
1962	69.1	69.3	70.1	71.0
1963	70.6	71.8	73.3	74.3
1964	75.1	76.9	77.6	78.8
1965	79.8	80.2	80.8	82.2
1966	82.9	83.9	83.1	83.3
1967	81.6	82.7	82.2	86.2
ORIGINAL DATA				
1966	78.8	82.8	83.6	87.9

Source: 1950-59: data for the Federal Republic from [2] are adjusted for the inclusion of West Berlin and the Saarland from [2].
1960-65: data including West Berlin and Saarland from [2].
First Quarter 1966: data including West Berlin and Saarland from [3, Viertes Heft 1967].
Second Quarter 1966-Fourth Quarter 1967: data including West Berlin and Saarland from [3, Erstes Heft 1968].

TABLE B7

Investment in Equipment, in Constant Deutsche Mark
[*Anlageinvestitionen, Ausruestung, Volumen,*
Preisbasis 1954=100]

(Quarterly, Billions of 1954 Deutsche Mark)

	1ST QUARTER	2ND QUARTER	3RD QUARTER	4TH QUARTER
SEASONALLY ADJUSTED				
1950	2.6	2.8	3.1	3.3
1951	3.3	3.3	3.2	3.3
1952	3.4	3.5	3.6	3.6
1953	3.7	3.8	3.9	4.0
1954	4.2	4.4	4.6	5.0
1955	5.2	5.5	5.8	5.9
1956	5.9	6.1	5.9	5.9
1957	5.9	5.8	5.8	6.0
1958	6.1	6.2	6.4	6.4
1959	6.4	6.7	7.1	7.6
1960	7.8	8.1	8.4	8.6
1961	9.1	9.2	9.1	9.3
1962	9.6	9.5	9.7	9.8
1963	9.6	9.7	10.3	10.3
1964	10.6	11.0	11.3	11.7
1965	12.1	12.2	12.2	12.4
1966	12.4	12.1	11.5	11.4
1967	10.3	10.3	10.5	12.2
ORIGINAL DATA				
1966	11.9	12.1	11.2	12.2

Source: 1950-59: data for the Federal Republic from [2] are adjusted for the inclusion of West Berlin and the Saarland from [2].
1960-65: data including West Berlin and Saarland from [2].
First Quarter 1966: data including West Berlin and Saarland from [3, Viertes Heft 1967].
Second Quarter 1966-Fourth Quarter 1967: data including West Berlin and Saarland from [3, Erstes Heft 1968].

TABLE B8

Investment in Construction, in Constant Deutsche Mark

[*Anlageinvestitionen, Bauten, Volumen, Preisbasis 1954=100*]

(Quarterly, Billions of 1954 Deutsche Mark)

	1ST QUARTER	2ND QUARTER	3RD QUARTER	4TH QUARTER
SEASONALLY ADJUSTED				
1950	2.8	2.7	2.8	2.9
1951	2.7	2.6	2.8	3.1
1952	3.0	2.8	3.0	3.1
1953	3.8	3.8	3.6	3.6
1954	3.5	4.0	4.2	4.4
1955	4.2	4.9	5.0	5.0
1956	5.1	5.3	5.2	5.3
1957	5.4	5.1	5.2	5.4
1958	5.1	5.5	6.0	6.1
1959	6.3	6.5	6.5	6.7
1960	7.0	6.7	6.6	6.9
1961	7.9	7.2	6.9	7.2
1962	7.6	7.6	7.6	7.2
1963	7.0	7.6	8.4	8.6
1964	8.6	8.9	8.7	9.2
1965	8.8	9.2	9.2	9.2
1966	9.9	9.5	9.3	9.3
1967	9.8	8.5	8.2	9.0
ORIGINAL DATA				
1966	7.3	10.0	10.4	10.2

Source: 1950-59: data for the Federal Republic from [2] are adjusted for the inclusion of West Berlin and the Saarland from [2].
1960-65: data including West Berlin and Saarland from [2].
First Quarter 1966: data including West Berlin and Saarland from [3, Viertes Heft 1967].
Second Quarter 1966-Fourth Quarter 1967: data including West Berlin and Saarland from [3, Erstes Heft 1968].

TABLE B9

Inventory Changes, in Constant Deutsche Mark
[*Anlageinvestitionen, Bauten, Volumen,
Preisbasis 1954=100*]
(Quarterly, Billions of 1954 Deutsche Mark)

	1ST QUARTER	2ND QUARTER	3RD QUARTER	4TH QUARTER
SEASONALLY ADJUSTED				
1950	0.8	1.3	1.1	1.0
1951	0.7	1.0	1.2	0.9
1952	1.6	1.1	0.9	1.4
1953	0.8	0.5	0.7	1.2
1954	0.9	1.2	0.9	1.3
1955	1.7	1.8	2.1	1.4
1956	1.6	1.9	1.4	1.6
1957	1.9	1.4	1.7	1.8
1958	1.5	0.9	1.2	1.0
1959	0.8	1.1	1.9	2.1
1960	1.9	2.3	2.1	2.1
1961	1.5	2.1	1.6	1.3
1962	1.1	0.8	0.1	1.2
1963	1.8	0.7	-0.3	-0.1
1964	0.5	1.4	2.1	2.0
1965	2.1	1.7	2.1	1.2
1966	1.0	0.9	0.0	0.0
1967	-2.7	-1.0	-0.3	0.6
ORIGINAL DATA				
1966	3.3	0.5	1.8	-3.6

Source: 1950-59: data for the Federal Republic from [2] are adjusted for the inclusion of West Berlin and the Saarland from [2].
1960-65: data including West Berlin and Saarland from [2].
First Quarter 1966: data including West Berlin and Saarland from [3, Viertes Heft 1967].
Second Quarter 1966-Fourth Quarter 1967: data including West Berlin and Saarland from [3, Erstes Heft 1968].

TABLE B10

Employee Income, After Taxes
[Nettoeinkommen, Loehne und Gehaelter]
(Quarterly, Billions of Deutsche Mark)

	1ST QUARTER	2ND QUARTER	3RD QUARTER	4TH QUARTER
SEASONALLY ADJUSTED				
1950	8.5	8.8	9.5	10.1
1951	10.5	10.9	11.3	11.6
1952	12.0	12.1	12.3	12.6
1953	12.9	13.4	13.9	14.0
1954	14.2	14.6	15.0	15.6
1955	16.0	16.6	17.2	17.6
1956	18.5	18.5	18.9	19.6
1957	20.2	20.3	20.5	21.0
1958	21.1	21.6	22.0	22.5
1959	22.8	23.2	23.8	24.5
1960	25.1	25.8	26.5	27.2
1961	28.6	29.2	29.5	29.9
1962	31.6	31.9	32.6	33.0
1963	33.4	34.4	35.2	35.4
1964	36.4	37.2	38.0	39.4
1965	40.5	41.8	42.4	43.4
1966	43.8	44.2	45.0	45.2
1967	44.4	43.7	44.3	45.1
ORIGINAL DATA				
1966	41.7	45.0	45.4	46.2

Source: 1950-59: data for the Federal Republic from [2] are adjusted for the inclusion of West Berlin and the Saarland from [2].
1960-65: data including West Berlin and Saarland from [2].
First Quarter 1966: data including West Berlin and Saarland from [3, Viertes Heft 1967].
Second Quarter 1966-Fourth Quarter 1967: data including West Berlin and Saarland from [3, Erstes Heft 1968].

TABLE B11

Disposable Income [*Verfuegbare Einkommen*]
(Quarterly, Billions of Deutsche Mark)

	1ST QUARTER	2ND QUARTER	3RD QUARTER	4TH QUARTER
SEASONALLY ADJUSTED				
1950	16.0	16.9	18.0	18.1
1951	19.0	19.7	20.6	21.0
1952	22.0	22.6	23.0	23.7
1953	24.1	24.9	25.6	26.2
1954	26.5	26.5	27.4	28.1
1955	28.7	29.7	30.7	31.5
1956	32.3	32.8	33.3	34.4
1957	35.4	37.1	37.7	37.9
1958	39.4	39.9	40.7	40.7
1959	41.6	42.8	43.9	43.5
1960	45.1	45.2	47.0	49.2
1961	50.3	50.9	51.5	53.1
1962	55.1	55.8	56.5	57.4
1963	57.3	59.0	61.1	62.0
1964	63.5	64.8	66.0	68.4
1965	70.3	72.4	73.7	75.1
1966	75.2	77.6	79.2	78.7
1967	79.6	79.4	78.8	80.6
ORIGINAL DATA				
1966	72.3	75.4	77.1	86.1

Source: 1950-59: data for the Federal Republic from [2] are adjusted for the inclusion of West Berlin and the Saarland from [2].
1960-65: data including West Berlin and Saarland from [2].
First Quarter 1966: data including West Berlin and Saarland from [3, Viertes Heft 1967].
Second Quarter 1966-Fourth Quarter 1967: data including West Berlin and Saarland from [3, Erstes Heft 1968].

TABLE B12

Property and Enterpreneurs' Income, Including Undistributed Profits, After Taxes [Gewinne] (Quarterly, Billions of Deutsche Mark)

	1ST QUARTER	2ND QUARTER	3RD QUARTER	4TH QUARTER
SEASONALLY ADJUSTED				
1950	5.2	5.7	6.5	6.6
1951	6.9	7.1	7.4	7.4
1952	8.0	8.1	7.9	8.4
1953	7.9	7.6	7.9	8.1
1954	8.3	8.5	8.8	9.3
1955	9.9	10.4	10.6	10.9
1956	10.9	11.2	11.1	11.3
1957	11.7	11.6	12.3	12.1
1958	12.5	12.9	13.2	12.2
1959	12.3	13.2	14.2	15.2
1960	16.0	15.5	15.1	15.4
1961	16.2	15.3	15.2	15.4
1962	15.1	15.7	15.8	15.9
1963	15.2	15.7	16.8	16.8
1964	17.2	17.8	18.3	18.9
1965	18.8	18.7	18.6	18.9
1966	18.7	19.4	18.9	21.2
1967	17.1	18.2	16.5	23.2
ORIGINAL DATA				
1966	15.6	18.0	19.5	25.6

Source: 1950-59: data for the Federal Republic from [2] are adjusted for the inclusion of West Berlin and Saarland from [2].
1960-65: data including West Berlin and Saarland from [2].
First Quarter 1966: data including West Berlin and Saarland from [3, Viertes Heft 1967].
Second Quarter 1966-Fourth Quarter 1967: data including West Berlin and Saarland from [3, Erstes Heft 1968].

TABLE B13

Industrial Production, Total, Excluding Construction

[Industrielle Nettoproduktion, Gesamte Industrie, Ohne Bauhauptgewerbe]

(Monthly, 1960 = 100)

	JAN	FEB	MAR	APR	MAY	JUN	JUL	AUG	SEP	OCT	NOV	DEC
SEASONALLY ADJUSTED												
1950	35	35	36	37	39	39	41	42	43	44	45	45
1951	46	47	47	48	48	48	49	48	48	48	49	48
1952	49	49	49	49	49	50	50	51	52	52	53	52
1953	53	53	54	55	55	56	55	57	58	58	58	59
1954	58	59	60	60	61	62	63	63	64	65	65	67
1955	68	68	69	69	70	72	72	73	74	74	75	76
1956	76	76	76	77	78	78	79	79	79	78	79	79
1957	80	81	79	82	83	82	82	81	83	83	83	82
1958	83	84	84	83	83	84	83	85	83	83	85	85
1959	85	85	87	85	88	88	88	92	92	94	94	95
1960	96	96	96	99	98	100	101	100	101	103	103	105
1961	106	106	107	106	106	104	105	106	107	107	106	109
1962	108	110	110	110	111	112	111	112	114	111	113	112
1963	110	112	112	113	113	115	115	117	117	118	120	119
1964	121	121	123	123	124	123	125	126	125	128	128	129
1965	130	131	131	132	132	132	131	132	133	134	132	133
1966	135	135	135	135	135	137	135	131	133	131	132	131
1967	129	128	127	128	128	128	129	128	133	134	136	137
ORIGINAL DATA												
1966	128	132	136	140	139	140	127	118	135	137	142	131

Source: 1950-54: data from [10], shifted to 1960 base by data from [11, 1964 issue, p. 243].
1955-September 1965: data from [7].
October 1965-67: data from [10], shifted to 1960 base by data from [11, 1965 issue, p. 246].

TABLE B14

Industrial Production, Investment Goods
[*Industrielle Nettoproduktion, Investitionsgueterindustrie*]
(Monthly, 1960 = 100)

	JAN	FEB	MAR	APR	MAY	JUN	JUL	AUG	SEP	OCT	NOV	DEC
SEASONALLY ADJUSTED												
1950	24	25	25	27	28	29	30	32	33	34	35	35
1951	37	37	38	38	38	39	40	39	39	39	40	41
1952	42	41	43	42	42	43	43	44	44	44	45	45
1953	45	45	45	45	45	45	45	47	47	47	48	49
1954	48	50	50	51	52	54	55	55	56	58	58	60
1955	61	62	63	64	65	66	68	68	69	70	70	70
1956	72	70	72	72	73	72	74	73	74	72	72	71
1957	74	77	73	76	75	76	74	75	77	76	76	76
1958	78	80	81	79	80	81	80	84	80	81	84	83
1959	81	82	83	80	83	84	84	89	88	93	92	92
1960	93	93	94	98	97	101	103	100	102	105	104	107
1961	109	109	110	109	108	106	110	108	109	108	108	113
1962	110	112	108	110	111	113	111	113	116	111	112	111
1963	110	108	113	112	110	114	114	116	117	116	120	118
1964	118	121	124	122	122	122	124	125	122	126	128	128
1965	135	134	129	131	133	133	130	131	132	133	130	131
1966	134	133	134	134	133	135	132	128	128	128	126	125
1967	120	118	118	117	117	116	118	118	124	124	126	128
ORIGINAL DATA												
1966	126	131	134	140	139	142	119	105	131	133	137	132

Source: 1950-54: data from [10], shifted to 1960 base by data from [11, 1964 issue, p. 243].
1955-September 1965: data from [7].
October 1965-67: data from [10], shifted to 1960 base by data from [11, 1965 issue, p. 246].

TABLE B15

Wages and Salaries, Manufacturing, Before Taxes

[*Lohn und Gehaltsumme in der Industrie, Brutto*]

(Monthly, Millions of Deutsche Mark)

	JAN	FEB	MAR	APR	MAY	JUN	JUL	AUG	SEP	OCT	NOV	DEC
SEASONALLY ADJUSTED												
1950	1,205	1,223	1,230	1,211	1,266	1,296	1,308	1,377	1,434	1,422	1,495	1,492
1951	1,549	1,580	1,627	1,645	1,715	1,748	1,723	1,768	1,770	1,775	1,812	1,784
1952	1,842	1,892	1,830	1,852	1,865	1,829	1,893	1,884	1,902	1,968	1,920	1,950
1953	1,975	1,953	1,984	2,034	2,008	2,044	2,094	2,067	2,096	2,124	2,084	2,149
1954	2,099	2,144	2,180	2,188	2,171	2,230	2,256	2,248	2,323	2,318	2,375	2,421
1955	2,377	2,429	2,510	2,520	2,528	2,609	2,538	2,669	2,716	2,674	2,780	2,808
1956	2,842	2,929	2,930	2,897	3,004	3,010	2,930	3,085	2,982	3,077	3,107	3,119
1957	3,159	3,168	3,135	3,189	3,263	3,177	3,248	3,266	3,213	3,260	3,299	3,245
1958	3,406	3,386	3,360	3,451	3,450	3,414	3,518	3,418	3,487	3,536	3,415	3,512
1959	3,503	3,475	3,494	3,580	3,522	3,632	3,690	3,591	3,759	3,800	3,808	3,918
1960	3,798	3,953	4,033	4,021	4,033	4,165	4,143	4,303	4,398	4,299	4,470	4,581
1961	4,484	4,552	4,674	4,553	4,723	4,741	4,676	4,798	4,786	4,800	4,933	4,906
1962	5,089	5,105	5,107	5,132	5,259	5,217	5,238	5,304	5,201	5,365	5,272	5,272
1963	5,485	5,331	5,409	5,483	5,599	5,475	5,610	5,534	5,578	5,730	5,642	5,668
1964	5,901	5,919	5,854	5,986	5,929	6,009	6,098	6,132	6,177	6,312	6,300	6,525
1965	6,411	6,580	6,616	6,718	6,665	6,792	6,835	6,827	6,986	6,860	7,037	7,041
1966	6,903	7,069	7,315	7,157	7,281	7,305	7,253	7,343	7,333	7,144	7,175	7,163
1967	7,025	6,972	6,954	6,938	6,924	6,985	6,854	6,994	6,899	6,992	7,061	6,957
ORIGINAL DATA												
1966	6,714	6,445	7,155	7,052	7,217	7,416	7,322	7,477	7,257	7,020	7,632	7,781

Source: 1950-59: data are the sum of data for the Federal Republic from [10] and for West Berlin from [12] . They are adjusted for the inclusion of the Saarland by data from [11] .

1960-61: data are the sum of data for the Federal Republic and for the Saarland both from [11] and for West Berlin from [12] .

1962-67: data including West Berlin and Saarland from [10] .

TABLE B16

Sales, Domestic, Manufacturing, Including Sales Taxes
[*Industrie, Inlandsumsatz*]
(Monthly, Millions of Deutsche Mark)

	JAN	FEB	MAR	APR	MAY	JUN	JUL	AUG	SEP	OCT	NOV	DEC
SEASONALLY ADJUSTED												
1951	8,344	8,536	8,151	8,611	8,303	8,401	8,132	8,565	8,644	8,763	9,071	9,073
1952	9,358	9,307	8,905	8,841	9,154	8,632	9,089	9,100	9,306	9,501	9,151	9,178
1953	9,352	9,183	9,603	9,531	9,171	9,772	9,755	9,593	9,802	9,874	9,774	9,858
1954	9,684	9,900	10,288	10,351	10,518	10,421	10,855	10,826	10,962	10,857	11,285	11,653
1955	11,477	11,868	12,250	12,081	12,296	12,647	12,491	13,011	13,229	12,892	13,180	13,613
1956	13,515	13,442	13,483	13,745	13,705	14,469	13,850	14,241	13,830	14,146	14,490	14,027
1957	14,668	14,757	14,434	14,723	15,031	14,898	15,001	14,966	14,838	15,147	15,107	14,790
1958	15,428	14,980	14,933	15,168	14,772	14,621	15,512	14,872	14,573	15,643	14,925	15,348
1959	15,106	15,415	15,259	15,864	16,185	16,805	16,902	16,511	17,442	17,191	17,339	18,024
1960	17,159	18,276	18,826	18,388	18,758	18,357	18,527	19,174	19,519	18,455	19,498	20,335
1961	20,075	20,185	20,683	20,022	19,964	20,605	19,801	20,598	20,424	20,094	20,746	20,442
1962	21,166	21,212	21,165	20,850	21,747	21,298	21,798	22,243	21,283	22,319	22,540	21,075
1963	21,773	21,098	21,254	22,496	22,493	22,462	22,848	22,311	22,603	23,458	22,628	22,450
1964	23,537	23,793	22,654	23,861	24,077	24,551	25,481	23,657	24,936	24,971	25,039	25,782
1965	25,103	25,986	26,528	26,365	25,972	25,526	26,232	26,193	26,820	26,168	26,936	27,531
1966	26,832	27,055	27,166	26,869	27,289	27,329	26,526	26,930	26,964	25,931	26,015	25,367
1967	25,680	25,161	25,063	25,241	24,686	25,761	25,253	25,617	25,357	26,574	26,635	27,988
ORIGINAL DATA												
1966	24,700	24,501	29,100	26,413	26,921	27,500	26,097	26,033	28,996	27,959	27,252	26,247

Source: 1951-61: data are sum of data for the Federal Republic and West Berlin both from [10] (West Berlin 1951 from [12]). They are adjusted for the inclusion of the Saarland by data from [11].
1962-63: data including West Berlin and Saarland from [11].
1964-67: data including West Berlin and Saarland from [10].

TABLE B17

Producers' Prices, Industrial Products

[*Erzeugerpreise, Industrielle Produkte*]

(Monthly, 1962 = 100)

	JAN	FEB	MAR	APR	MAY	JUN	JUL	AUG	SEP	OCT	NOV	DEC
ORIGINAL DATA												
1950	79.6	79.6	78.8	78.0	78.0	78.0	78.0	78.8	79.6	80.3	81.1	84.3
1951	88.3	91.5	93.9	94.7	95.5	94.7	93.9	94.7	94.7	95.5	97.8	97.8
1952	97.1	97.1	96.3	97.1	96.3	97.1	96.3	96.3	97.1	96.3	96.3	96.3
1953	95.5	96.3	95.5	94.7	94.7	93.9	92.9	93.1	93.1	93.1	93.1	93.1
1954	92.3	92.3	92.3	92.3	92.3	92.3	92.3	92.3	92.3	93.1	93.1	93.1
1955	93.9	94.1	94.2	94.1	94.3	94.5	94.6	94.8	94.9	94.8	95.0	95.2
1956	95.4	95.6	95.8	95.6	95.5	95.3	95.2	95.3	95.4	96.2	97.0	97.5
1957	98.0	98.0	97.9	97.8	97.6	97.5	97.4	97.4	97.3	97.4	97.4	97.6
1958	97.8	97.7	97.6	97.5	97.2	97.2	97.0	97.0	96.9	96.9	96.9	96.9
1959	96.6	96.5	96.4	96.2	96.2	96.1	96.1	96.4	96.5	96.8	97.0	97.0
1960	97.1	97.1	97.0	97.1	97.2	97.2	97.4	97.7	98.0	98.2	98.4	98.5
1961	98.8	98.9	98.8	98.8	98.7	98.6	98.7	98.9	99.0	99.2	99.2	99.3
1962	99.5	99.6	99.7	100.0	100.0	100.0	100.0	100.1	100.2	100.2	100.3	100.3
1963	100.5	100.6	100.5	100.4	100.3	100.3	100.3	100.4	100.5	100.6	100.7	100.8
1964	100.9	101.0	101.1	101.2	101.2	101.2	101.2	101.5	101.9	102.4	102.8	102.7
1965	103.0	103.4	103.5	103.8	104.0	104.0	104.1	104.2	104.4	104.7	104.6	104.8
1966	105.3	105.7	105.9	106.2	106.2	106.1	106.2	105.8	105.7	105.7	105.7	105.6
1967	105.6	105.5	105.4	104.7	104.6	104.7	104.7	104.7	104.5	104.5	104.7	104.8

Source: 1950-54: data from [11], shifted to 1962 base by data from [11, 1961 and 1964 issues].

1955-57: data from [10, Nov. 1961 issue], shifted to 1962 base by data from [10, Feb. 1965 issue and 11, 1964 issue].

1958-67: data from [10].

TABLE B18

Stock Prices, Industry [*Aktienkurse, Industrie*]
(Monthly, 1960 = 100)

	JAN	FEB	MAR	APR	MAY	JUN	JUL	AUG	SEP	OCT	NOV	DEC
ORIGINAL DATA												
1950	9	9	8	8	8	8	8	9	9	9	9	9
1951	10	11	11	11	11	11	12	13	14	15	17	17
1952	19	19	17	17	16	15	15	15	15	15	14	14
1953	14	14	13	13	13	13	13	14	15	16	16	16
1954	16	17	17	17	17	18	20	21	22	23	24	26
1955	28	28	29	32	32	32	33	34	34	31	30	31
1956	32	30	31	31	30	29	29	28	29	29	28	29
1957	29	28	29	29	29	28	29	30	31	30	30	31
1958	32	32	32	33	33	35	35	38	40	43	45	45
1959	48	48	48	51	55	61	63	78	74	70	74	78
1960	80	81	80	82	89	102	111	122	121	116	110	107
1961	106	104	102	104	110	110	103	95	90	92	98	94
1962	92	90	89	86	79	72	70	67	66	61	67	70
1963	68	66	65	67	73	75	74	77	79	78	76	76
1964	81	83	87	86	85	83	85	86	87	84	81	81
1965	82	80	78	78	76	74	73	74	74	72	71	69
1966	71	72	71	71	68	64	60	60	62	60	59	59
1967	58	62	63	63	62	62	62	70	73	74	77	79

Source: 1950-54: data from [10, April 1956 issue], shifted to 1960 base by data from [11, 1961 issue].
1955-September 1965: data from [7].
October 1965-66: data from [10], shifted to 1960 base by data from [11, 1961 issue].
1967: data from [10], shifted to 1960 base by data from [10, July 1967 issue].

TABLE B19

Imports of Raw Materials, Industrial [*Einfuhr, Gewerbliche Halbwaren*]

(Monthly, Million Deutsche Mark)

	JAN	FEB	MAR	APR	MAY	JUN	JUL	AUG	SEP	OCT	NOV	DEC
SEASONALLY ADJUSTED												
1950	211	217	210	238	244	273	310	312	300	361	368	389
1951	388	436	458	439	433	420	438	440	503	428	481	473
1952	498	478	485	442	444	425	487	464	434	485	420	476
1953	454	406	411	448	470	488	434	424	446	423	466	413
1954	399	401	453	462	456	470	443	468	473	477	507	490
1955	539	577	589	592	584	600	620	660	691	645	650	683
1956	671	668	644	686	704	702	708	714	734	741	726	751
1957	753	791	824	826	852	818	840	789	761	795	775	730
1958	724	700	663	632	603	607	632	638	631	632	633	618
1959	619	617	624	625	647	667	681	672	670	684	708	753
1960	723	754	774	760	761	750	742	762	770	773	792	790
1961	802	771	774	793	770	771	755	734	740	748	732	716
1962	750	753	744	745	752	749	722	777	728	718	719	739
1963	730	706	798	785	795	806	827	827	800	817	825	814
1964	850	887	887	913	869	880	922	883	934	940	967	985
1965	969	938	914	903	953	970	927	958	990	950	982	970
1966	981	1,004	1,007	1,012	1,017	1,004	1,003	992	955	994	916	945
1967	925	923	926	915	916	928	971	1,008	1,055	1,090	1,142	1,117
ORIGINAL DATA												
1966	1,042	943	1,098	934	1,041	1,009	1,039	978	932	961	896	977

Source: 1950-67: data including West Berlin from [10].

January 1950-June 1959: adjusted for the inclusion of the Saarland by data from [9, supplement, December 1960 from 13].

TABLE B20

Imports of Semimanufacturers, Industrial [*Einfuhr, Gewerbliche Halbwaren*]
(Monthly, Million Deutsche Mark)

	JAN	FEB	MAR	APR	MAY	JUN	JUL	AUG	SEP	OCT	NOV	DEC
SEASONALLY ADJUSTED												
1950	115	99	89	117	104	125	111	150	160	181	192	175
1951	161	169	176	169	163	158	182	179	167	157	158	172
1952	214	235	205	184	188	182	199	170	198	210	200	235
1953	186	204	187	190	191	194	195	250	225	225	230	226
1954	214	247	272	269	310	330	303	297	332	318	365	367
1955	391	405	427	448	449	460	442	452	400	415	402	439
1956	434	433	429	443	449	447	444	465	435	431	479	475
1957	498	499	488	507	521	473	507	487	493	497	492	467
1958	484	451	441	425	435	436	469	442	471	489	462	456
1959	437	437	453	460	474	486	488	516	555	548	546	598
1960	585	670	697	653	685	680	685	674	666	702	695	675
1961	737	652	646	678	624	645	574	629	600	570	590	619
1962	662	642	647	646	647	623	661	682	664	685	673	641
1963	596	615	694	693	716	701	703	693	662	716	685	665
1964	716	792	666	758	746	800	861	806	861	854	880	942
1965	962	896	889	908	905	922	889	852	921	856	899	900
1966	819	916	962	880	940	877	888	937	910	942	886	861
1967	859	864	821	846	829	907	848	942	921	955	1,053	1,087
ORIGINAL DATA												
1966	825	810	944	840	905	932	947	932	898	991	893	899

Source: 1950-67: data including West Berlin from [10].
January 1950-June 1959: adjusted for the inclusion of the Saarland by data from [9, supplement, December 1960. from 13].

Index